Haydn Richards

Junior English 4

New Edition

Ginn is an imprint of Pearson Education Limited, a company incorporated in England and Wales, having its registered office at Edinburgh Gate, Harlow, Essex, CM20 2JE. Registered company number: 872828

www.ginn.co.uk

Text ©Haydn Richards, 1965

Revised edition 1997
This edition 2008

British Library Cataloguing in Publication Data is available from the British Library on request.

ISBN 978 0 435996 85 7

Typeset and illustrated by Planman Technologies India Pvt. Ltd.
Original illustrations ©Pearson Education Ltd, 2008
Cover design by Tony Richardson
Cover illustration ©Pearson Education Ltd, 2008

Acknowledgements
Every effort has been made to contact copyright holders of material reproduced in this book.
Any omissions will be rectifi ed in subsequent printings if notice is given to the publishers.

page 6–7 **Attacked by a crow**
Watership Down by Richard Adams, published by Penguin Books.
By kind permission of David Higham Associates Ltd.

page 12–13 **Toad and company**
The Wind in the Willows by Kenneth Grahame, copyright under the Berne Convention, reproduced by kind permission of Curtis Brown, London.

page 24 **Rikki-tikki and Darzee**
The Jungle Book by Rudyard Kipling.
By kind permission of A P Watt Ltd on behalf of The National Trust.

page 30 **William's Workshop**
William's Workshop by Susan Gates, published by Ginn and Company.
By kind permission of David Higham Associates Ltd.

page 48–49 **Insidethevault**
The Ghost ofThomas Kempe by Penelope Lively, published by William Heinemann Ltd.
By kind permission of Reed Consumer Books Ltd.

page 54 **A pony for Jody**
The Red Pony by John Steinbeck, published by William Heinemann Ltd.
By kind permission of Reed Consumer Books Ltd.

page 66 **Tarka fi ghts Deadlock**
Tarka the Otter by Henry Williams, published by The Bodley Head Ltd.
By kind permission of Random House UK Ltd.

page 78 **Johann Gutenberg**
Twenty Inventors by Jacqueline Dineen, published by Wayland Publishers Ltd.

page 84 **A fightinasignal-tower**
The Eagle ofthe Ninth by Rosemary Sutcliff, published by Oxford University Press.

PREFACE

This new edition of Haydn Richards' popular series is for pupils studying in primary schools. Based on the revised 1997 edition, this new edition retains the excellent coverage of spelling, punctuation and grammar topics in each of the four books, as well as the wide range and varying complexity of the reading comprehension and vocabulary exercises.

In this new edition, key spelling, punctuation and grammar points and their examples are always highlighted in boxes on the page for quick and easy reference.

The Publisher

CONTENTS

NOUNS

The **butcher** gave the **dog** a big meaty **bone**.

Butcher is the name of a **person**.
Dog is the name of an **animal**.
Bone is the name of a **thing**.

A noun is the name of a person, animal or thing.

(A) Make a list of the nouns shown in the picture below.

(B) Find the nouns in these sentences and write them down.

1 The car skidded on the ice and hit a tree.
2 Diamonds, rubies and emeralds are precious stones.
3 There are eleven players in a soccer team.
4 A dog is sometimes called "man's best friend".
5 The chief city of a country is called the capital.
6 The heart pumps blood to the body.
7 Rust is caused by oxygen in the air.
8 The referee ordered the offending player off the field.

(C) Complete the nouns with missing letters.

1 A r _ _ _ _ _ _ _ _ _ is a place where you can buy and eat a meal.
2 A h _ _ _ _ _ _ _ _ is a kind of plane capable of rising straight up from the ground and hovering in the air.
3 An artist mixes colours on a p _ _ _ _ _ .
4 A tr _ _ _ _ _ _ has three sides and three angles.
5 A d _ _ _ _ _ is a banknote used in the United States of America.

VERBS

Jamal **washed** his face and **brushed** his hair.

The words **washed** and **brushed** are verbs.

A verb is a word which shows action.

apologize	bewilder	comprehend	confess	confide
demolish	devour	discuss	expose	extinguish
fortify	glare	hibernate	inhale	loathe
meditate	pester	relax	strive	unite

(A) Make a list of the verbs in these sentences.

1 Fish breathe through their gills.
2 Many animals hibernate during the winter.
3 Some of them wake and search for food on mild days.
4 After digging the garden, Dad raked it well.
5 Brazil produces and exports vast quantities of coffee.
6 The ship struck an iceberg and sank.

(B) Copy the verbs in the column on the left, then opposite each write the meaning from the list below which matches it. Use your dictionary to help.

1 to breathe in
2 to eat like an animal
3 to become less stiff or firm
4 to tell as a secret
5 to spend the winter asleep
6 to uncover; to lay open
7 to express regret
8 to put out; to wipe out
9 to work hard or try hard
10 to understand
11 to make strong
12 to pull or tear down
13 to annoy; to irritate
14 to stare in anger
15 to confuse completely
16 to think quietly
17 to own up to a sin
18 to join together
19 to talk over
20 to regard with disgust

ADJECTIVES

> *The captain had a **brown bushy** beard.*
>
> The words **brown** and **bushy** describe the captain's beard.
>
> **A word which describes a noun is called an adjective.**
>
> | | | | | |
> |---|---|---|---|---|
> | arrogant | boisterous | contemptuous | distinguished | elaborate |
> | frantic | gorgeous | hospitable | intelligent | laborious |
> | memorable | obstinate | pompous | ponderous | prosperous |
> | radiant | repulsive | stagnant | stationary | tumultuous |

(A) Make a list of the adjectives in these sentences.

1 Rabbits become tame and affectionate when kept as pets.
2 Fruit for jam-making must be ripe, dry and clean.
3 The Canadian prairies are vast plains where huge quantities of wheat are grown.
4 Tame mice are sociable but quarrelsome creatures.
5 The otter has short legs, webbed toes and thick fur.
6 To withstand rough winds, lighthouses are built of interlocking blocks of masonry.

(B) Copy the adjectives in the column on the above. Opposite each write the meaning from the list below which matches it. Use your dictionary to help.

1 richly coloured; splendid
2 giving a warm welcome
3 very scornful
4 requiring much work
5 boastfully proud
6 successful; thriving
7 well-known; famous
8 heavy and clumsy
9 bright; shining
10 quick at learning
11 self-important
12 not moving
13 very noisy and disorderly
14 worked out with great care
15 not running or flowing
16 stubborn
17 rough; excited
18 causing strong dislike
19 not to be forgotten
20 wild with rage or pain

ADVERBS

1 *The troops fought **gallantly**.*

   Gallantly tells **how** the troops fought. (*manner*)

2 *We looked **everywhere** for the lost ball.*

   Everywhere tells **where** we looked. (*place*)

3 *We looked for the lost ball **yesterday**.*

   Yesterday tells **when** we looked. (*time*)

A word which describes how, where or when an action is performed is called an adverb.

awkwardly	*bitterly*	*contentedly*	*courageously*	*frugally*
gracefully	*hungrily*	*intimately*	*merrily*	*mournfully*
patiently	*politely*	*soundly*	*uproariously*	*violently*

(A) Make a list of the adverbs in these sentences. After each write **how**, **where** or **when** as required.

1 Nigel washed the dishes carefully.
2 Diana calls to see us frequently.
3 All the rabbits ran away.
4 The two boys wandered aimlessly round the town.
5 The train will be arriving shortly.
6 Dozens of rooks were cawing noisily.

(B) Complete each sentence by using a suitable adverb from the column on the above. Use your dictionary to help.

1 The thief struggled _____.
2 We waited _____.
3 The robin chirped _____.
4 The child wept _____.
5 The old man fell _____.
6 The champion fought _____.
7 The miser lives _____.
8 He ate his food _____.
9 The cows grazed _____.
10 He raised his hat _____.
11 The wind howled _____.
12 We all laughed _____.
13 The girls danced _____.
14 The baby slept _____.
15 I know him _____.

SINGULAR AND PLURAL NOUNS

Singular	Plural		Singular	Plural
chiefchief	ox	oxen		
chimney	chimneys		photo	photos
deer	deer		piano	pianos
diary	diaries		potato	potatoes
disco	discos		sheafsheaves	
factory	factories		shelf	shelves
goose	geese		son-in-law	sons-in-law
hero	heroes		thiefthieves	
man	men		turkey	turkeys
mouse	mice		wolfwolves	

s (in left margin)

(A) Write the plurals of these words.

1 piano	**6** diary	**11** deer
2 sheaf	**7** goose	**12** disco
3 chimney	**8** photo	**13** factory
4 hero	**9** thief	**14** son-in-law
5 mouse	**10** chief	**15** man

(B) Write the missing words.

1 factory	many ＿＿＿	**6** wolf	a pack of ＿＿＿
2 turkey	a flock of ＿＿＿	**7** piano	four ＿＿＿
3 chief	two ＿＿＿	**8** deer	a herd of ＿＿＿
4 potato	a sack of ＿＿＿	**9** ox	a team of ＿＿＿
5 thief	a gang of ＿＿＿	**10** mouse	three ＿＿＿

(C) Rewrite these sentences, changing the nouns in bold type to the plural number and making any other changes which may be necessary.

1 The **thief** removed the **turkey** from the **shelf**.
2 The **chief** put away his **knife**.
3 The **hero** had his **photo** taken.
4 The **child** looked at the little white **mouse**.
5 The **fox** looked longingly at the **goose**.

ATTACKED BY A CROW

The strange fragrance was stronger now, coming over the top of the rise in a wave of scent that struck him powerfully – as the scent of orange-blossom in the Mediterranean strikes a traveller who smells it for the first time. Fascinated, he ran to the crest. Nearby was another hedgerow and beyond, moving gently in the breeze, stood a field of broad beans in full flower.

Hazel squatted on his haunches and stared at the orderly forest of small, glaucous trees with their columns of black-and-white bloom. He had never seen anything like this. Wheat and barley he knew, and once he had been in a field of turnips. But this was entirely different from any of those and seemed, somehow, attractive, wholesome, propitious.

True, rabbits could not eat these plants: he could smell that. But they could lie safely among them for as long as they liked, and they could move through them easily and unseen. Hazel determined then and there to bring the rabbits up to the beanfield to shelter and rest until the evening. He ran back and found the others where he had left them. Bigwig and Silver were awake, but all the rest were still napping uneasily.

"Not asleep, Silver?" he said.

"It's too dangerous, Hazel," replied Silver. "I'd like to sleep as much as anyone, but if we all sleep and something comes, who's going to spot it?"

"I know. I've found a place where we can sleep safely for as long as we like."

"A burrow?"

"No, not a burrow. A great field of scented plants that will cover us, sight and smell, until we're rested. Come out here and smell it, if you like."

Both rabbits did so. "You say you've seen these plants?" said Bigwig, turning his ears to catch the distant rustling of the beans.

"Yes, they're only just over the top. Come on, let's get the others moving before a man comes with a *hrududu** or they'll scatter all over the place."

Silver roused the others and began to coax them into the field. They stumbled out drowsily, responding with reluctance to his repeated assurance that it was "only a little way".

They became widely separated as they struggled up the slope. Silver and Bigwig led the way, with Hazel and Buckthorn a short distance behind. The rest idled along, hopping a few yards and then pausing to nibble or to pass droppings on the warm, sunny grass.

* *hrududu* is rabbit talk for car or tractor

Silver was almost at the crest when suddenly, from half-way up, there came a high screaming – the sound a rabbit makes, not to call for help or frighten an enemy, but simply out of terror. Fiver and Pipkin, limping behind the others, and conspicuously undersized and tired, were being attacked by the crow. It had flown low along the ground. Then, pouncing, it had aimed a blow of its great bill at Fiver, who just managed to dodge in time. Now it was leaping and hopping among the grass tussocks, striking at the two rabbits with terrible darts of its head. Crows aim at the eyes and Pipkin, sensing this, had buried his head in a clump of rank grass and was trying to burrow farther in. It was he who was screaming.

Hazel covered the distance down the slope in a few seconds. He had no idea what he was going to do and if the crow had ignored him he would probably have been at a loss. But by dashing up he distracted its attention and it turned on him. He swerved past it, stopped and, looking back, saw Bigwig come racing in from the opposite side. The crow turned again, struck at Bigwig and missed. Hazel heard its beak hit a pebble in the grass with a sound like a snail-shell when a thrush beats it on a stone. As Silver followed Bigwig, it recovered itself and faced him squarely. Silver stopped short in fear and the crow seemed to dance before him, its great, black wings flapping in a horrible commotion. It was just about to stab when Bigwig ran straight into it from behind and knocked it sideways . . .

Watership Down   Richard Adams

1 In what way was the scent of the beanfield like the scent of orange-blossom in the Mediterranean?
2 What colour are the broad bean flowers?
3 Give two reasons why it would be safe for the rabbits to sleep in the beanfield.
4 Which two rabbits had been keeping watch while the younger rabbits tried to sleep?
5 Which rabbit was the closest to the beanfield when the crow attacked Pipkin and Fiver?
6 Why had the crow chosen Pipkin and Fiver for attack?
7 With what did the crow aim at Fiver?
8 How did Pipkin attempt to escape the crow's attack?
9 Who ran to Pipkin's aid?
10 In what way did this action assist Pipkin?
11 To what does the writer compare the sound made by the crow's beak on the pebble?
12 Which two creatures stood face to face in this fight?
13 What stopped the crow from stabbing at Silver?

VERBS PAST TENSE AND PAST PARTICIPLES

Remember

The **past tense** of a verb does **not** need a helping word (an auxiliary verb).

Example

*All the ponds **froze** last night.*

The **past participle** always requires an auxiliary verb.

Example

*All the ponds are **frozen** this morning.*

Auxiliary verbs

is	*are*	*was*	*were*	*has*	*have*
having	*had*	*be*	*been*	*being*	*am*

Present tense	**Past tense**	**Past participle**	**Present tense**	**Past tense**	**Past participle**
bear	*bore*	*borne*	*go*	*went*	*gone*
beat	*beat*	*beaten*	*hang* (thing)	*hung*	*hung*
begin	*began*	*begun*	*hang* (person)	*hanged*	*hanged*
blow	*blew*	*blown*	*hurt*	*hurt*	*hurt*
break	*broke*	*broken*	*lay*	*laid*	*laid*
burst	*burst*	*burst*	*lie*	*lay*	*lain*
choose	*chose*	*chosen*	*mistake*	*mistook*	*mistaken*
deal	*dealt*	*dealt*	*show*	*showed*	*shown*
drive	*drove*	*driven*	*slay*	*slew*	*slain*
drown	*drowned*	*drowned*	*think*	*thought*	*thought*
fight	*fought*	*fought*	*weave*	*wove*	*woven*
flee	*fled*	*fled*	*wring*	*wrung*	*wrung*
freeze	*froze*	*frozen*			

(A) In each sentence below insert the **past tense** of the verb in bold.

1 Tom and John _____ a gruelling fight. **fight**
2 The defeated army _____ before their pursuers. **flee**
3 The gladiator _____ his opponent with his sword. **slay**
4 On reaching home Veronica _____ the table for tea. **lay**
5 Dad _____ his hand with an electric drill. **hurt**
6 The spider _____ a web in a very short time. **weave**
7 His teacher _____ him for his twin brother. **mistake**
8 Vast floods _____ hundreds of sheep yesterday. **drown**

B Copy each sentence and complete it by inserting the **past participle** of the verb in bold type.

1 We rested after our visitors had _____. **go**
2 He had _____ of a good answer to the question. **think**
3 Several passengers were _____ in the collision. **injure**
4 David was _____ to captain the school team. **choose**
5 This lovely scarf was _____ by hand. **weave**
6 The condemned man was _____ at eight o'clock in the morning. **hang**
7 Margaret did the sum after her teacher had _____ her the right method. **show**
8 The ground was _____ so the match was postponed. **freeze**

C Insert in each space either the **past tense** or the **past participle** of the verb in bold type, as required.

1 The patient _____ the pain without flinching. **bear**
2 The old ship is to be _____ up next month. **break**
3 Many trees were _____ down during the gale. **blow**
4 Work was _____ on the new school yesterday. **begin**
5 The winner _____ the racing car skilfully. **drive**
6 Our team will probably be _____ in the final. **beat**
7 After lunch Grandma _____ down to rest. **lie**
8 Barbara washed the towel and _____ it out. **wring**

SENTENCES, CLAUSES AND PHRASES

Look at this group of words.
Mr Dobbin bought a new sports car yesterday.

Does it make complete sense? Yes.
Does it contain a verb? Yes

Then it is a **sentence**.

A sentence is **a group of words which makecompletesense** . Every sentence contains a **verb**.

Look at this group of words.
Which had new tyres?

Does it make complete sense? No.
Does it contain a verb? Yes.

Then it is a **clause**.

Look at this group of words.
Without even a glance at his book

Does it make complete sense? No.
Does it contain a verb? No.

Then it is a **phrase**.

(A) Say whether each group of words is a sentence, a clause or a phrase.

1 Most trees shed their leaves every autumn.
2 Early in the autumn of every year
3 Whenever they can
4 Most people work.
5 The farmer chased the boys.
6 Who were very frightened
7 Dogs with long hair and broad feet
8 Dogs bark.

(B) Form a sentence from each clause and phrase below.

1 .... at the bus stop.
2 .... because she is very fond of chocolates.
3 With one shot ....
4 Although he was very ill ....
5 .... on our doorstep every morning.
6 .... whenever she can.
7 With great pride..
8 ....who has climbed Mount Everest.
9 .... who are bullies..............................
10 Thinking quickly ....

NOUNS: GENDER

Masculine	Feminine	Masculine	Feminine
boar	sow	marquis	marchioness
brother	sister	mayor	mayoress
buck	doe	nephew	niece
bull	cow	peacock	peahen
colt	filly	ram	ewe
drake	duck	sir	madam
emperor	empress	stag	hind
heir	heiress	stallion	mare
host	hostess	widower	widow
husband	wife	wizard	witch
lord	lady		

(A) Write the **feminine** gender of:

1 sir	**3** lord	**5** peacock	**7** marquis	**9** nephew
2 stallion	**4** mayor	**6** emperor	**8** bull	**10** heir

(B) Write the **masculine** gender of:

1 duck	**3** widow	**5** hind	**7** niece	**9** doe
2 sow	**4** witch	**6** filly	**8** ewe	**10** empress

(C) In each sentence change the **masculine** noun to the **feminine** gender. You may need to change other words too.

1 The Emperor had twenty sons.
2 A beautiful peacock strutted about the lawn.
3 The driver of the bus was a young man.
4 The rich uncle sent a handsome present to his nephew.
5 The marquis is cruising in the Mediterranean.
6 The letter began, "Dear Sir".

(D) Complete each sentence by using a noun of the opposite gender to that in bold type.

1 Farmer Bond keeps two **bulls** and eight _____.
2 The **drake** swam on the pond while the _____ waddled round the farmyard with her little ones.
3 A record price was paid for the _____ and the **cow**.
4 **Lord** and _____ Bryce were at the garden party.
5 The wool on the **ram** was thicker than that on the _____.
6 The red deer **stag** had antlers; the _____ had none.

TOAD AND COMPANY

When they were quite ready the now triumphant Toad led his companions to the paddock and set them to capture the old grey horse, who, without having been consulted, and to his own extreme annoyance, had been told off by Toad for the dustiest job in this dusty expedition. He frankly preferred the paddock, and took a great deal of catching. Meantime Toad packed the lockers still tighter with necessaries, and hung nose-bags, nets of onions, bundles of hay, and baskets from the bottom of the cart. At last the horse was caught and harnessed, and they set off, all talking at once, each animal either trudging by the side of the cart or sitting on the shaft, as the humour took him. It was a golden afternoon. The smell of the dust they kicked up was rich and satisfying; out of thick orchards on either side of the road birds called and whistled to them cheerily; good-natured passers-by gave them "Good day," or stopped to say nice things about their beautiful cart; and rabbits, sitting at their front doors in the hedgerows, held up their fore-paws and said, "O my! O my! O my!"

Late in the evening, tired and happy and miles from home, they drew up on a remote common far from habitations, turned the horse loose to graze, and ate their simple supper sitting on the grass by the side of the cart. Toad talked big about all he was going to do in the days to come, while stars grew fuller and larger all around them, and a yellow moon, appearing suddenly and silently from nowhere in particular, came to keep them company and listen to their talk. At last they turned into their little bunks in the cart; and Toad, kicking out his legs, sleepily said, "Well, good night, you fellows! This is the real life for a gentleman! Talk about your old river!"

"I *don't* talk about my river," replied the patient Rat. "You *know* I don't, Toad. But I *think* about it," he added pathetically, in a lower tone: "I *think* about it – all the time!"

The Mole reached out from under his blanket, felt for the Rat's paw in the darkness, and gave it a squeeze. "I'll do whatever you like, Ratty," he whispered. "Shall we run away tomorrow morning, quite early – *very* early – and go back to our dear old hole on the river?"

"No, no, we'll see it out," whispered back the Rat. "Thanks awfully, but I ought to stick by Toad till this trip is ended. It wouldn't be safe for him to be left to himself. It won't take very long. His fads never do. Good night!"

The end was indeed nearer than even the Rat suspected.

After so much open air and excitement the Toad slept very soundly, and no amount of shaking could rouse him out of bed next morning. So the Mole and Rat turned to, quietly and manfully, and while the Rat saw to the horse, and lit a fire, and cleaned last night's cups and platters, and got things ready for breakfast, the Mole trudged off to the nearest village, a long way off, for milk and eggs and various necessaries the

Toad had, of course, forgotten to provide. The hard work had all been done, and the two animals were resting, thoroughly exhausted, by the time Toad appeared on the scene, fresh and gay, remarking what a pleasant easy life it was they were all leading now, after the cares and worries and fatigues of housekeeping at home.

The Wind in the Willows   Kenneth Grahame

1 What job did Toad give Rat and Mole to do while he packed the lockers?
2 What made Rat and Mole's job difficult to do?
3 What did Toad hang from the bottom of the cart?
4 What were the animals doing when they were not trudging by the side of the cart?
5 Where did Toad and his friends stop for the night?
6 What did they do with the horse?
7 Where did they eat their supper?
8 Write down one word that means the same as **talked big** in the second paragraph.
9 How do we know that Rat is feeling a little homesick?
10 Why doesn't he leave Toad and go straight home?
11 Who sets off to buy what they need for breakfast?
12 Do you think Rat and Mole would agree with Toad when he comments on the "pleasant easy life" they are leading?
13 Write down five adjectives that would describe Toad accurately on the evidence of this extract from *The Wind in the Willows*.

ADJECTIVES: FORMATION

Some adjectives are formed simply by adding the letter **y** to a noun.
Examples cloud cloudy   mould   mouldy   marsh   marshy
When the noun ends with **e**, this letter is dropped before the **y** is added.
Examples shade   shady   smoke   smoky   juice   juicy
When **y** is added to some nouns the last letter is doubled.
Examples   sun   sunny   mud   muddy   star   starry

(A) Use the adjective formed from the noun in bold type to fill each space. Copy the phrases in your book.

1 A material covered with **fluff**   a ＿＿ material
2 A voice with a **squeak**   a ＿＿ voice
3 Foods containing much **starch**   ＿＿ foods
4 A man of great **wealth**   a ＿＿ man
5 A morning with much **frost**   a ＿＿ morning

(B) Insert in each space the adjective formed from the noun in bold type. Remember to drop the final **e**.

1 A path with many **stones**   a ＿＿ path
2 Hair in which there is a **wave**   ＿＿ hair
3 Dishes covered with **grease**   ＿＿ dishes
4 A day when a **breeze** is blowing   a ＿＿ day
5 A dinner with a nice **taste**   a ＿＿ dinner
6 A beach covered with **pebbles**   a ＿＿ beach

(C) Form the adjective from the noun in bold type to fill each space. Remember to double the final letter.

1 An animal covered with **fur**   a ＿＿ animal
2 A sound like that of **tin**   a ＿＿ sound
3 Wood full of **knots**   ＿＿ wood
4 Land which is largely **bog**   ＿＿ land
5 A speech containing much **wit**   a ＿＿ speech
6 A hand which is more **skin** than flesh   a ＿＿ hand

(D) Form the adjective from the noun in bold type. You need to remember all the rules for forming adjectives for this exercise.

1 roads covered in **ice**   ＿＿ roads
2 hair like **wire**   ＿＿ hair
3 a complexion with **spots**   a ＿＿ complexion
4 sunshine through **haze**   ＿＿ sunshine
5 a beach of **sand**   a ＿＿ beach
6 a morning of **fog**   a ＿＿ morning

NOUNS: FORMATION

Verb	Noun	Verb	Noun
abolish	abolition	astonish	astonishment
advise	advice	complain	complaint
choose	choice	deceive	deceit
complete	completion	destroy	destruction
decide	decision	explode	explosion
explain	explanation	imagine	imagination
favour	favouritism	inquire	inquiry
improve	improvement	pursue	pursuit
pronounce	pronunciation	satisfy	satisfaction
accuse	accusation		

The nouns here are all **abstract nouns**. They are the names of ideas and feelings.

(A) Copy these phrases, inserting in the spaces the nouns formed from the verbs in bold type.

1 a lively _____   **imagine**   6 complete _____   **astonish**
2 sound _____   **advise**   7 a sensible _____   **decide**
3 a violent _____   **explode**   8 correct _____   **pronounce**
4 widespread _____   **destroy**   9 a false _____   **accuse**
5 blatant _____   **favour**   10 a serious _____   **complain**

(B) Complete each sentence by inserting the noun formed from the verb in bold type.

1 Purchasers have a _____ of several colours.   **choose**
2 In 1833 an Act was passed for the _____ of slavery in the British Empire.   **abolish**
3 Any _____ to increase pensions will be welcomed.   **decide**
4 He listened patiently to his teacher's _____.   **explain**
5 The work was done to the customer's _____.   **satisfy**
6 Several hunters went in _____ of the lion.   **pursue**
7 An _____ is a search for truth, knowledge or information.   **inquire**
8 The work on the new road is nearing _____.   **complete**
9 _____ means making a person believe to be true something which is false.   **deceive**
10 The _____ in Jake's written work was amazing.   **improve**

OTHER WORDS FOR SAID AND ASKED

Using **said** or **asked** too often makes your writing monotonous.

admitted	announced	boasted	remarked
shouted	stammered	urged	whispered

A Choose the most suitable word from the above list to complete each sentence.

1 "It is much colder today than it was yesterday," _____ the old boatman.
2 "Hush, Becky," _____ her mother, "or you will wake the baby."
3 "Go on, Samran," _____ his teacher, "try to beat David's jump."
4 "All hands on deck," _____ the skipper of the trawler.
5 "I b-b-beg your pardon," _____ the frightened boy.
6 "Yes, it was I who broke the basin," _____ Kai Man.
7 "I am easily the best reader in the class," _____ Alan.
8 "The school will be closed all next week," _____ the headmaster.

complained	grumbled	inquired	ordered
pleaded	prophesied	protested	replied

B Choose the most suitable word from the above list to complete each sentence.

1 "Prepare the theatre for an emergency operation at once," _____ the surgeon.
2 "Is this the way to the Post Office, please?" _____ the stranger.
3 "Yes," _____ the policeman, "keep straight on for about fifty metres and you will see it on your left."
4 "Please, Mum, may I have just one more chocolate?" _____ Elizabeth.
5 "Your prices are far too high," _____ the customer to the grocer.
6 "I think we are going to have a very warm summer this year," _____ Aunt Jane.
7 "Your dog has been worrying my sheep, Mr Bath," _____ the farmer.
8 "I get all the tedious jobs," _____ the shop assistant.

COLLECTIVE NOUNS

Noun	Collective	Noun	Collective
actors	company	minstrels	troupe
angels	host	pilgrims	band
arrows	sheaf; quiver	singers	choir
bells	peal	spectators	crowd
chicks	brood	stars	cluster; galaxy
directors	board	swallows	flight
eggs	clutch	teachers	staff
golf-clubs	set	thieves	gang
lions	pride	trees	clump
locusts	plague; swarm	worshippers	congregation
magistrates	bench		

(A) Write the missing words.

1 a _____ of singers

2 a _____ of teachers

3 a _____ of chicks

4 a _____ of bells

5 a _____ of actors

6 a _____ of locusts

7 a _____ of spectators

8 a _____ of thieves

9 a _____ of lions

10 a _____ of swallows

11 a host of _____

12 a clump of _____

13 a cluster of _____

14 a band of _____

15 a board of _____

16 a troupe of _____

17 a quiver of _____

18 a bench of _____

19 a congregation of _____

20 a clutch of _____

(B) Write the collective nouns needed to complete these sentences.

1 The _____ of pilgrims halted before the mosque.

2 A _____ of locusts devoured every growing plant.

3 The mother hen was accompanied by her _____ of chicks.

4 Under a small _____ of trees a tent had been pitched.

5 Several plays have been performed by this brilliant _____ of actors.

6 The police are searching for a _____ of car thieves.

7 The _____ of directors met to consider their company's losses.

8 The match was watched by a huge _____ of spectators.

9 In his dream Jacob saw a _____ of angels.

10 The children saw a _____ of swallows making for the sea.

11 The _____ in the tiny chapel prayed silently.

12 My grandfather was given a _____ of golf-clubs when he retired.

WILDLIFE IN DANGER

It is a disturbing fact that today many different kinds of wild animal throughout the world are in danger of extinction. The reasons for this are many and varied, but we must largely blame pollution, pesticides, the disturbance of the animals' natural environment and man's greed and thoughtlessness.

Industry has grown enormously, and it has become common practice for factories to dispose of waste matter in streams and rivers, causing great loss of river life. Modern agricultural methods include the use of pesticides which effectively control insects classified as pests, but which also destroy many that are not. An increase in population has meant more building – and with it the destruction of much of the countryside that provides habitat for wild animals. To satisfy man's selfish desires the polar bear in North America is under threat, hunted by sportsmen; in Borneo and Sumatra the orang–utan has become part of a smuggling racket; in South America the chinchilla is almost extinct because its fur is in demand; whales are massacred world-wide for the oil and food they yield. These are only a few of the species under threat.

But the problem is receiving world-wide recognition, and some action is being taken. To name a few examples – sewage pollution in the River Thames has been greatly reduced; a ban on trading in some furs has been agreed; and organisations like Friends of the Earth do valuable work in this deserving cause.

1 Give in your own words two reasons why some species of wild animal may become extinct.
2 How do factories contribute to the problem?
3 What is the meaning of **pesticide**?
4 What effect has the increase in the human population had upon wildlife?
5 Why is the polar bear in North America under threat?
6 Which countries have problems with smuggling?
7 Which animal is hunted for its fur?
8 Why are whales hunted in such large numbers?
9 What is being done to help preserve our river life?
10 Name one other way in which wildlife is currently helped.
11 Provide a subtitle for each paragraph that will sum up what each is about.

FUN WITH WORDS

a _ _ _ _	a male farm animal	Word (**a**) is bull
b _ _ _ _ _ _	a missile fired from a rifle	Word (**b**) is bullet

Now try the exercise below. Remember that each dash stands for a letter, and that the second word of each pair is formed by adding letters to the first word.

(A)

1 a _ _ _ _   a large stringed instrument
   b _ _ _ _ _ _ _   a spear used in hunting whales

2 a _ _ _ _   a man who lives in a monastery
   b _ _ _ _ _ _   an agile and mischievous animal

3 a _ _ _   a young goat
   b _ _ _ _ _ _   to steal a person by force

4 a _ _ _   an article of headgear
   b _ _ _ _ _ _ _   a small axe

5 a _ _ _ _   an American coin of small value
   b _ _ _ _ _ _   the middle

6 a _ _ _ _   a place where ships can shelter
   b _ _ _ _ _ _ _   a part or a share

7 a _ _ _ _   stop
   b _ _ _ _ _ _   a rope or strap for leading an animal

8 a _ _ _ _   a man who entertains guests
   b _ _ _ _ _ _ _   of an enemy; unfriendly

9 a _ _ _   a male child
   b _ _ _ _ _ _ _   to refuse to have anything to do with

10 a _ _ _ _   a lump; a large quantity together
    b _ _ _ _ _ _ _ _ wholesale pitiless slaughter

(B) In a certain code the figures stand for the word

5	2	9	7	4	6	3	1	8
C	O	M	P	A	N	I	E	S

Write the words for:
1 8 5 4 9 7
2 5 2 9 1 8
3 7 4 6 3 5
4 8 6 3 7 1
5 8 7 4 5 1

Write the figures for:
6 C A P E S
7 O P E N S
8 S P I C E
9 P I A N O
10 S C O N E

USING THE RIGHT ADJECTIVE

shrewd	vivid	candid	riotous	abundant
luscious	secluded	righteous	sumptuous	prosperous

(A) Copy the adjectives in column **a** in your exercise book in the order given. Opposite each write the noun in column **b** which matches it.

a	b	a	b
frantic	slope	injurious	daughter
antique	allowance	threadbare	struggles
affectionate	drugs	meagre	task
formidable	grip	precipitous	furniture
palatable	clothes	relentless	meal

(B) Choose the word from the list above which will complete each sentence correctly.

1 The traveller had many _____ memories of his jungle adventures.
2 The peach is a _____ fruit.
3 Sir Walter is the managing director of a _____ business.
4 The _____ businessman made a profit.
5 A _____ feast was held in the emperor's honour.
6 The boys were rocking with _____ laughter.
7 The town is proud of its _____ supply of water.
8 He gave them his _____ opinion of their actions.
9 At the bottom of the garden was a _____ nook with an oak seat beneath a shady tree.
10 The insult filled the woman with _____ indignation.

PRONOUNS

a *John told Susan that John would lend Susan a book.*

b *John told Susan that **he** would lend **her** a book.*

Instead of repeating the word John, the word **he** is used in (**b**).

Instead of repeating the word **Susan**, the word **her** is used.

A word which is used instead of a noun is called a pronoun.

he	*it*	*she*	*her*
we	*us*	*his*	*him*

myselfitself   yourselves   herself
yourselfourselves   them   they

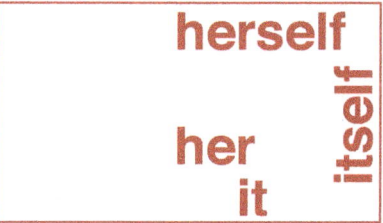

A Rewrite these sentences, using pronouns from the list above in place of the words in bold type.

1 Anne told Justine that **Anne** would knit a cardigan for **Justine**.
2 When Colin was given a dog **Colin** trained **thedog** to walk to heel.
3 Ramu and I are good friends. **Ramu and I** go everywhere together.
4 As Roger and I approached the farmyard gate a big them dog barked at **Roger and me**.
5 The teacher sent for Robin and Alan. **The teacher** told **Robin and Alan** to stay in after school.
6 The two girls knew that **thetwo girls** would be late.
7 Andrew was sad because the stolen bicycle was **Andrew's**.

B Insert one of the pronouns in the list above in each sentence.

1 You boys must make _____ useful in the garden.
2 Did you make this table _____, Spencer?
3 The hedgehog can roll _____ into a prickly ball.
4 I can work out the sum by _____, thank you.
5 Leela certainly thinks _____ somebody of importance.
6 We built the house _____.

HOMOPHONES

Some words are pronounced like other words but are different in spelling and meaning, e.g. *main, mane*   *bear, bare*.

Such words are called homophones.

air	what we breathe	**cereal**	wheat, barley and oats are all cereals
heir	one entitled to a dead person's property		
		serial	a story appearing in parts
allowed	permitted	**check**	to stop; a squared pattern
aloud	loud enough to be heard	**cheque**	an order to a bank to pay money
beach	the sea-shore		
beech	a tree	**coarse**	rough
boy	a male child	**course**	a track; an onward movement
buoy	a floating marker for ships		
brake	a device to check speed	**currant**	a dried grape
break	to cause something to come into pieces	**current**	a flow of water, air, etc.
		foul	filthy; wicked; vile
		fowl	a bird

(A) Choose the correct word from the pair above to complete each sentence.

1 cereal   serial
Cornflakes are his favourite _____.

2 currant   current
These _____ buns are delicious.

3 foul   fowl
Real Madrid were awarded a free-kick for a _____ on their goalkeeper.

4 air   heir
The King's son was _____ to the throne.

5 break   brake
New blocks had to be fitted to the front _____ of the bicycle.

(B) Write five pairs of words to complete these sentences.

1 Dad paid by _____ for his new _____ suit.
2 The _____ who fell overboard swam to a nearby _____.
3 Talking _____ is not _____ in the reading room of the library.
4 Racing was difficult because the grass on the _____ was long and _____.
5 Not far from the sandy _____ grew a clump of _____ trees.

ABBREVIATIONS

Abbreviations are shortened forms of words or phrases.

Learn this list, then do the exercises.

AA	Automobile Association	**NSPCC**	National Society for the Prevention of Cruelty to Children
asap	as soon as possible		
c/o	care of		
Dept	Department	**OHMS**	On Her Majesty's Service
HRH	His (Her) Royal Highness	**RN**	Royal Navy
JP	Justice of the Peace	**RSPCA**	Royal Society for the Prevention of Cruelty to Animals
Ltd	Limited		
MD	Managing Director		
MP	Member of Parliament	**UN**	United Nations
n/a	not applicable; not available	**Tel**	Telephone

(A) Write the meanings of the abbreviations in bold type.

1 The widow wrote to her **MP** about her compensation.
2 The letter was addressed to the Sales **Dept**.
3 An inspector of the **NSPCC** called to inspect the house.
4 Tim's holiday address is **c/o** Mrs Baines, 15 High St., Burland.
5 A large crowd gathered to greet **HRH** Princess Margaret.
6 The matter has been reported to the **RSPCA**.
7 Please reply **asap**.
8 The warrant for the arrest of the culprit was signed by a **JP**.

(B) Give the meaning of each abbreviation in bold type.

1 On the notepaper was printed: **Tel** Bury 2385.
2 No postage is payable on letters and parcels sent **OHMS**.
3 The building of the **RN**. Barracks at Devonport was begun in 1879.
4 The **AA** was founded in London in 1905.
5 Both Britain and America are members of the **UN**.
6 Mum's company has a new **MD**.

(C) Use your dictionary to find out what these abbreviations stand for.

1 fax   2 GP   3 R.I.P   4 anon.   5 HQ

RIKKI-TIKKI AND DARZEE

Then Rikki-tikki went out into the garden to see what was to be seen. It was a large garden, only half-cultivated, with bushes as big as summer-houses of Marshal Niel roses, lime and orange trees, clumps of bamboo, and thickets of high grass. Rikki-tikki licked his lips. "This is a splendid hunting-ground," he said, and his tail grew bottle-brushy at the thought of it, and he scuttled up and down the garden, snuffing here and there till he heard very sorrowful voices in a thornbush.

It was Darzee, the tailor-bird, and his wife. They had made a beautiful nest by pulling two big leaves together and stitching them up the edges with fibres, and had filled the hollow with cotton and downy fluff. The nest swayed to and fro, as they sat on the rim and cried.

"What is the matter?" asked Rikki-tikki.

"We are very miserable," said Darzee. "One of our babies fell out of the nest yesterday, and Nag ate him."

"H'm!" said Rikki-tikki. "That is very sad – but I am a stranger here. Who is Nag?"

Darzee and his wife only cowered down in the nest without answering, for from the thick grass at the foot of the bush there came a low hiss – a horrid cold sound that made Rikki-tikki jump back two clear feet. Then inch by inch out of the grass rose up the head and spread hood of Nag, the big black cobra, and he was five feet long from tongue to tail.

The Jungle Book   Rudyard Kipling

1 Why did Rikki-tikki lick his lips?
2 What change came over Rikki-tikki's tail as he thought about this?
3 What did Rikki-tikki hear as he scuttled up and down the garden?
4 Explain why tailor-bird is an appropriate name for these birds.
5 Why were Darzee and his wife crying?
6 Where did the low hiss come from?
7 What did Darzee and his wife do when they heard this noise?
8 What effect did this sound have on Rikki-tikki?
9 How long was Nag from tongue to tail?
10 Write a list of all the facts about the cobra in this passage.

LETTER WRITING

Alastair Brooks saw this advertisement in a magazine.

FREE

The REX packet of 100 foreign stamps to applicants for our approval sheets and illustrated catalogue.

Enclose stamp for postage.
Rex Stamp Co. Ltd., 146 Forsyth Rd.,
London NW5 2BQ

Rex Stamp Co. Ltd.,   19 Jubilee Road,
146 Forsyth Road,   Granton,
London   Kent
NW5 2BQ   GN7 4CP

Dear Sirs

Please send me the Rex free packet of foreign stamps, also a selection of approval sheets and a copy of your illustrated catalogue.

I enclose stamps for postage.

Yours faithfully,

Alastair Brooks.

Rex Stamp Co. Ltd.,
146 Forsyth Road,
London
NW5 2BQ

This is how he addressed the envelope.   This is the letter he wrote.

Points to remember:

a   Keep to the form of letter shown, giving your full address.
b   State exactly what you require, making your letter as brief as possible.
c   If requested to enclose stamps or a postal order, make sure you do so.
d   Address the envelope plainly and fully, and see that it bears stamp for the correct postage.

1   Write a letter to the Planet Novelty Co. Ltd, 49 Greenham Avenue, London E12 SA16 for a copy of their price-list of conjuring tricks, enclosing stamps for postage.
2   The Medico Co. Ltd., Grove Buildings, Anson Street, Birmingham B12 4EH, offer a free sample tube of Atlas toothpaste to all applicants enclosing stamps for postage. Send for a sample.
3   Write to the Mekko Model Co. Ltd., 37 Bilton Road, London SE16 8RL for a copy of their illustrated catalogue of model railways, aircraft, racing cars and boats, which will be sent post free.

OCCUPATIONS

software designer	plumber	librarian	newsagent
chef	butcher	cricketer	undertaker
florist	chemist	coastguard	upholsterer
nurse	waitress	glazier	tailor
jeweller	steeplejack		

A Write the names of these occupations from the list above.

B Select the word from the list above which will complete each sentence.

1 The _____ at the public library has three excellent assistants.

2 The _____ at the corner sells lots of different sweets and chocolates.

3 The _____ at the beach café served us with tea very quickly.

4 The _____ had a large selection of medicines and pills.

5 The _____ offered Maya a gold watch at a reduced price.

6 The twins went to the _____ to buy their mother a bouquet of flowers.

7 The _____ displays all the meat on trays in the shop window.

8 The _____ climbed to the top of the church steeple to inspect the damage done by the gale.

9 The _____ alerted the lifeboat crew.

10 The _____ took Tom's temperature and pulse every four hours.

GROUP NAMES

baker	alligator	villa
silver	synagogue	venison

(A) Choose the word in the column above which belongs to each of the groups below. Give the name of each group.

Example   **1 venison**   names of meats

1 beef
chicken
lamb
mutton

2 house
bungalow
mansion
cottage

3 cathedral
temple
church
chapel

4 copper
gold
iron
lead

5 cobra
crocodile
adder
lizard

6 grocer
butcher
fruiterer
fishmonger

(B) Draw four columns and write the headings:

Clothes   Vessels   Furniture   Footwear

Then place the words below in their correct groups. There will be six words in each group.

liner	sandals	tights	wardrobe
clogs	submarine	boots	trousers
cupboard	scarf	sideboard	cruiser
shirt	armchair	yacht	cabinet
trawler	shoes	vest	wellingtons
table	schooner	slippers	jeans

(C) Give the name of the group to which these objects belong.

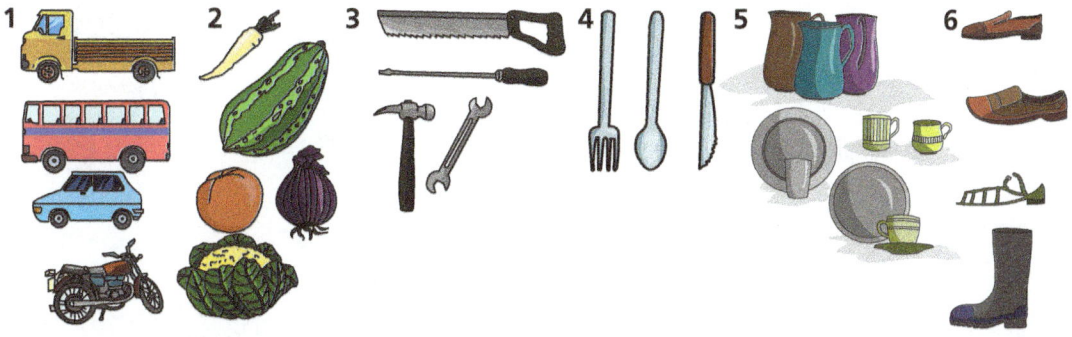

1   2   3   4   5   6

COMPARING ADJECTIVES

There are **three** degrees of adjectives.

The **positive degree**.
Used for one person or thing e.g. *tall*

The **comparative degree**.
Used in comparing two persons or things e.g. *taller*

The **superlative degree**.
Used in comparing more than two persons or things e.g. *tallest*

We can add **-er** and **-est** to many adjectives without any change in spelling, e.g. strong, stronger, strongest.

But look out for these spelling changes.

a Dropping final **e**. e.g. *fast, faster, fastest*

b Changing **y** to **i**. e.g. *happy, happier, happiest*

c Doubling the last letter. e.g. *hot, hotter, hottest.*

When comparing longer adjectives the words **more** and **most**, or **less** and **least** are placed before them.

Example
*Jill is the **most reliable** person for the job.*

(A) Copy and complete this table.

Positive degree	Comparative degree	Superlative degree
1 lovely	_____	_____
2 large	_____	_____
3 hot	_____	_____
4 noisy	_____	_____
5 slim	_____	_____
6 wise	_____	_____
7 wet	_____	_____
8 wealthy	_____	_____
9 fine	_____	_____
10 greedy	_____	_____

B Complete each sentence, using the **comparative degree** or the **superlative degree** of the adjective in bold type.

1 Sanjay is the _____ pupil of the two.   **capable**
2 She is easily the _____ girl in the whole school.   **intelligent**
3 Julian is the _____ of the two brothers.   **generous**
4 Janna chose the _____ dress in the shop.   **expensive**
5 A miner's work is _____ than a farmer's.   **dangerous**
6 Many people consider the Taj Mahal to be the _____ building in the world.   **wonderful**
7 The manager has the _____ job in the works.   **important**
8 This is the _____ book of the two.   **interesting**

Some adjectives cannot be compared in the ways shown; they are irregular.

Positive degree	Comparative degree	Superlative degree
good	better	best
bad	worse	worst
ill	worse	worst
many	more	most
much	more	most
little	less	least

C Write the correct degree of the adjective which will complete each sentence.

1 This is the _____ blizzard I have ever seen.   **bad**
2 The patient was very ill yesterday but he is even _____ today.   **ill**
3 Both boys read well, but David is the _____ reader.   **good**
4 Your cold is _____ than mine.   **bad**
5 £1 is the _____ amount that can be invested.   **small**
6 August is the month when guest-houses have the _____ bookings.   **many**
7 Kate is the _____ singer in the school choir.   **good**
8 Ahmed has little money; Paul has even _____.   **little**

WILLIAM'S WORKSHOP

SCENE 1 **Onthe way home from school**

Characters: LAURA, DANNY, WILLIAM

(William enters, looking fearfully behind him. He has a school bag on his back. He is followed by Danny and Laura.)

LAURA: Wimpy William! Wimpy William!

DANNY: He'll run away in a minute. Just watch him. Why don't you run away, wimp?

WILLIAM: I won't run away.

LAURA: Oh! He's being brave today. Go on, tell us about your workshop again, William. Tell us what you make in there.

DANNY: *(Sarcastically)* Didn't you know? William makes incredible things in there. He makes computers that talk to you and do your homework. And robot dogs that bark and fetch your slippers. He makes all sorts of wonderful stuff in there. He's a brilliant genius, an inventor. At least, that's what he's always telling us.

LAURA: *(Sarcastically)* Oh, I didn't know that. I didn't know he was a genius. I thought he was a little wimpy baby who can't fight, who runs away. I thought he was a daydreamer, like teacher says.

DANNY: And I thought he was a great big liar – who says he's inventing things in his workshop when he isn't.

WILLIAM: It's true, it's true. I do invent things. But they don't always work. I mean, I never said they worked, did I?

LAURA: He's making excuses now!

WILLIAM: I'm not, I'm just . . .

DANNY: *(Interrupting)* Well, I think it's about time we saw one of these wonderful inventions. Go on, William, bring in your latest invention. Bring it to school tomorrow.

WILLIAM: Well, I would do. Honest I would. But my latest invention is really big. It's too big to bring into school. And anyway, it's not finished yet.

LAURA: More excuses! He's just trying to wriggle out of it!

DANNY: So what is this big invention then, William? Is it a space rocket or something? A rocket that'll fly you to Mars?

WILLIAM: *(Quietly)* Don't be silly. I couldn't make one of those in my workshop.

DANNY: (Not listening) Because if it's a space rocket you could fly it to school, William. Fly it to school and land on the football field!

LAURA: Anyway, your workshop's not even a proper workshop. It's just a crumbly old garden shed!

William's Workshop Susan Gates

1 Where is William going when the scene opens?

2 Why do you think he looks "fearfully" behind him?

3 What is William's workshop?

4 Danny teases William by naming three inventions that William may or may not have tried to make. What are they?

5 Do you consider that Danny and Laura are bullying William? Give your reasons.

6 Why do you think Laura and Danny are behaving in this way?

7 How do you think William feels?

8 Do you think William is a "wimp" on the basis of the evidence in the passage?

9 Give the meaning of these words as they are used in the passage.
   sarcastically   incredible   robot

10 What do you learn about Laura in this passage? Use the evidence in the passage to support what you say.

11 How would you like this play to end? Suggest a satisfying ending.

WRITING A PLAYSCRIPT

When you write a playscript, remember these points:

a No inverted commas are used for speech.
b Names of speakers are written in capital letters on the left.
c A colon (:) separates the names of the speakers from what they say.
d Special instructions to the actors (stage directions) are written in brackets.

Spot the differences in punctuation and layout between this conversation presented first as direct speech and then in playscript form.

Direct speech
Nervously Mrs Jones asked, "May I come in?"
"Of course you can, my dear," replied Mrs White.
"Come straight in and sit yourself down."
"Oh, thank you!" said Mrs Jones, almost in tears.

Playscript
MRS JONES: (Nervously) May I come in?

MRS WHITE: Of course you can, my dear. Come straight in and sit yourself
                down.

MRS JONES: (Almost in tears) Oh, thank you!

(A) Turn to the extract from *The Jungle Book* on page 24. Write out the conversation between Rikki-tikki and Darzee as a playscript.

(B) Write a conversation between members of your family as a playscript.

(C) Write one of these conversations in playscript form:

   1 An argument about which television programme to watch.
   2 A telephone conversation between two schoolfriends.
   3 A teacher telling a pupil to work harder and a pupil protesting.
   4 Two friends on a fishing trip.

(D) Rewrite the last five speeches of
William's Workshop (pages 30 and 31)
as direct speech.

PEOPLE

exile	A person banished from his or her native country
genius	An exceptionally brainy or gifted person
hypocrite	Pretends to be better than he or she really is
lunatic	A person who is mad
mimic	Imitates the voice and actions of others
pedestrian	Travels about on foot
prophet	Foretells coming events
traitor	Betrays his or her country, friends or any trust
tyrant	Uses his or her power to oppress others
vandal	Wilfully damages or destroys property

(A) Give one word for each of the following.

1 A person who gives to charity regularly yet leads an evil life in secret.
2 Someone who sells his or her country's secrets to a foreign power.
3 A king who treats his subjects harshly.
4 A person who is not in his or her right mind.
5 A person who has not seen his or her native land for many years.

(B) Complete each sentence by using a word from the list.

1 The event was foretold by a _____.
2 A _____ who crossed the road without looking both ways was knocked down by a car.
3 Shakespeare, who wrote some of the world's best plays, was a _____.
4 A _____ had uprooted shrubs in the park and smashed several windows in the pavilion.
5 The _____ gave wonderful imitations of the people around him.

PROPER ADJECTIVES

A **proper adjective** is one formed from a **proper noun**, which is the name of a particular person, place or thing.

Alps	*Alpine*	*Holland*	*Dutch*	*Portugal*	*Portuguese*
Belgium	*Belgian*	*Iceland*	*Icelandic*	*Spain*	*Spanish*
China	*Chinese*	*Israel*	*Israeli*	*Sweden*	*Swedish*
Cyprus	*Cypriot*	*Malta*	*Maltese*	*Switzerland*	*Swiss*
Denmark	*Danish*	*Mexico*	*Mexican*	*Turkey*	*Turkish*
Finland	*Finnish*	*Norway*	*Norwegian*	*Venice*	*Venetian*
Greece	*Greek*	*Poland*	*Polish*		

(A) Copy these phrases, inserting in each the **proper adjective** formed from the proper noun in bold type.

1 A _____ dance **Spain**
2 A _____ goddess **Greece**
3 _____ glass **Venice**
4 A _____ restaurant **China**
5 _____ bulbs **Holland**
6 _____ oranges **Israel**
7 A _____ cross **Malta**
8 The _____ fiords **Norway**
9 An _____ village **Alps**
10 _____ timber **Sweden**

(B) Complete each sentence below by using a **proper adjective** from the list above.

1 Matthew is staying on a small _____ island. **Greece**
2 Tampico is a _____ port. **Mexico**
3 Hercule Poirot is a famous _____ detective created by Agatha Christie. **Belgium**
4 _____ watches are renowned for their reliability. **Switzerland**
5 A fez is a felt cap with a long tassel formerly worn by _____ men. **Turkey**
6 _____ wines are famous, the best known being Port Wine. **Portugal**
7 Thousands of fish were caught by the _____ trawlers. **Iceland**
8 The long narrow boats used on _____ canals are called gondolas. **Venice**
9 The gentian is a beautiful _____ flower. **Alps**
10 The _____ word "suomi" means "fish-scale". **Finland**

NOUNS: POSSESSION

To make a **singular** noun show possession add **'s**.

Examples

the computer belonging to Mum   *the beak ofthe duck*
Mum's computer   *the duck's beak*

(A) Make these examples into singular nouns.

   1 the dress belonging to Ann   **6** the jaws of the lion
   2 the sword belonging to the knight   **7** the reward of the winner
   3 the thimble belonging to the tailor **8** the gloves of the boxer
   4 the shop belonging to the butcher   **9** the jokes of the comedian
   5 the pads belonging to the cricketer

To make a **plural** noun **ending with s** show possession add **'**.

Examples

the football belonging to the boys   *the necks ofthe swans*
the boys' football   *the swans' necks*

(B) Make these examples into possessive plurals.

   1 the trousers belonging to the   **4** the bones belonging to the dogs
       clowns   **5** the toys belonging to the girls
   2 the tusks belonging to the   **6** the tails of the monkeys
       elephants   **7** the wings of the insects
   3 the uniforms belonging to the   **8** the nests of the birds
       sailors   **9** the cloakroom for ladies

To make a **plural** noun **which does not end with s** show possession, add **'s** just
as with a singular noun.

Examples

the work ofthe men   *fashions for women*
the men's work   *women's fashions*

(C) Make these examples into possessive plurals.

   1 handbags for women   **5** toys for children
   2 the yokes belonging to the oxen   **6** shoes for men
   3 the tails belonging to the mice   **7** the camp of the airmen
   4 the helmets belonging to the   **8** the feet of the frogmen
       policemen   **9** the honks of the geese

SEA-LIONS

Sea-lions bear some resemblance to seals, though they are much larger. When fully grown they are from twelve to twenty feet in length, and from eight to fifteen feet in circumference; they are extremely fat, so that having cut through the skin, which is about an inch in thickness, there is at least a foot of fat before you come to either lean or bones.

Their skins are covered with short grey hair, but their tails and their fins, which serve them for feet on shore, are almost black. They have a distant resemblance to an overgrown seal, though in some particulars there is a manifest difference between them, especially in the males. These have a large snout, or trunk, hanging down five or six inches below the end of the upper jaw, which the females have not.

These animals divide their time equally between the land and the sea, continuing at sea all the summer, and coming on shore at the setting in of winter, where they reside during the whole of that season. In this interval they bring forth their young, and have generally two at a birth, which they suckle with their milk, they being at first about the size of a full-grown seal. During the time these sea-lions continue on shore, they feed on the grass and small plants which grow near the banks of fresh-water streams.

They often, especially the males, have furious battles with each other, principally about their females; and we were one day surprised by the sight of two sea-lions goring each other with their teeth until they were covered with blood.

Anson's Voyage Round the World   Richard Walter

1 Which is the bigger, a sea-lion or a seal?
2 What is the length of a fully grown sea-lion?
3 What is the thickness of a sea-lion's skin?
4 What thickness of fat lies between the skin of a sea-lion and its flesh or bones?
5 What purpose is served by the sea-lion's tail and fins when it is on shore?
6 Where does the sea-lion spend the summer?
7 Where does it spend the winter?
8 At what time of year are young sea-lions born?
9 How does the face of a male sea-lion differ from that of a female?
10 What do the male sea-lions fight about, chiefly?

CONTRACTIONS

Can't is a short way of writing **cannot**.

I'll is a short way of writing **I will**.

These shortened forms are called **contractions**. Now see how the word **would** is used in contractions.

I would	*I'd*	*you would*	*you'd*	*he would*	*he'd*
she would	*she'd*	*we would*	*we'd*	*they would*	*they'd*

(A) In each sentence write a contraction in place of the words in bold type.

1 The police said **they would** be glad of the information.
2 Our teacher asked us if **wewould** like to have a concert.
3 I think **you would** be interested in this book.
4 Dad said **hewould** give me a football next week.
5 Mum promised **shewould** help me to swim.
6 The doctor told me **I would** be better in a few days.

(B) Write the contractions for the following.

1 I am	**8** shall not	**15** are not
2 you have	**9** we have	**16** you are
3 she is	**10** it is	**17** we would
4 will not	**11** have not	**18** they have
5 he would	**12** she will	**19** cannot
6 do no	**13** I would	**20** they will
7 they are	**14** we are	

(C) Write the words for which the contractions stand.

1 **I can't** forget that **I'm** bereft Of all the pleasant sights they see.
The Pied Piper ofHamelin

2 Said Francis then, "Faith, gentlemen, **we're** better here than there."
The Glove and the Lions

3 The old sage said, "**You're** as sound as a nut."
The Enchanted Shirt

4 Out spoke a wife: "**We've** beds at home; **We'll** burn them for a light?"
The Wives ofBrixham

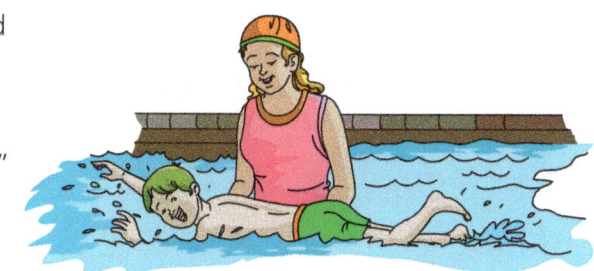

ANTONYMS: OPPOSITES

	Opposite		Opposite			Opposite
absent	present	false	true	poverty	wealth
admit	deny	hollow	solid	proud	humble
advance	retreat	hurry	loiter	seldom	often
arrival	departure	ignorance	knowledge	shallow	deep
bold	timid	innocent	guilty	superior	inferior
cheap	expensive	joy	sorrow	wild	tame
conceal	reveal	miser	spendthrift	win	lose
danger	safety	permit	forbid		
failure	success	plentiful	scarce		

A Write the **opposites** of the following words.

1 joy	**6** ignorance	**11** bold	**16** poverty
2 miser	**7** innocent	**12** proud	**17** hurry
3 cheap	**8** advance	**13** false	**18** conceal
4 admit	**9** hollow	**14** plentiful	
5 permit	**10** arrival	**15** failure	

B Complete each sentence by inserting the **opposite** of the word in bold type.

1 Mum's new coat was quite **cheap**, but her shoes were very _____.
2 Nine members were **present** and three were _____.
3 Some of the defendant's statements were **true**, but many were _____.
4 Megan dived in at the **deep** end; Kayleigh paddled at the _____ end.
5 Sally always **hurries** home from school but Carol often _____ on the way.
6 Kevin is **innocent** but everyone knows that his brother is _____.

C In each column find the **two antonyms** or opposites. Use your dictionary to help you.

1 curious	**4** timid	**7** bright
violent	simple	apathetic
guilty	huge	light
innocent	bold	enthusiastic
2 plentiful	**5** happiness	**8** stop
superior	poverty	forget
scarce	thrift	pay
brilliant	wealth	start
3 attack	**6** unknown	**9** acquire
forbid	heavy	sell
receive	famous	purchase
permit	popular	gamble

DIRECT AND INDIRECT SPEECH

Direct speech	Indirect speech
"Have you cleaned your teeth, Nigel?" asked his mother.	*Nigel's mother asked him ifhe had cleaned his teeth.*
The sentence contains the **exact words** spoken by Nigel's mother.	This sentence does not contain the exact words spoken by Nigel's mother.
Direct speech always requires inverted commas, or speech marks, " "	Indirect speech does not require inverted commas.

(A) Change to **indirect speech**.

1 "Can I have a bicycle for my birthday?" asked Matthew.
2 "I have a bad headache, so I think I will lie down," said Mr Dean.
3 "The days are certainly getting longer," remarked Mr Caldwell.
4 "Do you know how to play darts, Roger?" asked David.
5 "You look as if you could do with a good holiday," said Mrs Smith to her son.
6 "Peter, tuck your shirt in!" ordered his mother.
7 "Come inside, Mrs Dale," invited the old lady, "and have tea with us."

(B) Change to **direct speech**.

1 The shoe repairer told Robert that his shoes would be ready by Saturday.
2 Simon's mother asked him if he had loitered on the way home from school.
3 Bernard's teacher asked him if he had ever spent a holiday in France.
4 Bernard replied that he had once been on a day trip to Dieppe.
5 The headmaster told the boys that their work was improving.
6 Judith told her father that she had come top in English.
7 Her father promised to give her ten pounds if she stopped biting her nails for three months.
8 My mother said that she was feeling tired.
9 I said that I should love to come.
10 The doctor advised me to stay home from school.

OPPOSITES: USING A PREFIX

The opposites of some words can be formed by writing before them **un**, **in**, **il**, **dis**, **ir** or **im**.

un	**in**	**dis**	**ir**
aware	considerate	appear	regular
certain	efficient	approve	responsible
favourable	equality	connect	reverent
fortunate	frequent	continue	
grateful	gratitude	courteous	**im**
important	human	honest	movable
kind	sane	obedient	patient
necessary		orderly	perfect
popular	**il**	regard	probable
usual	legal	similar	proper

(A) Form the opposites of these words, using prefixes.

1 sane	**5** obedient	**9** certain	**13** continue
2 aware	**6** approve	**10** perfect	**14** considerate
3 human	**7** equality	**11** gratitude	**15** orderly
4 usual	**8** similar	**12** regard	

(B) Select a word from the list to complete each sentence.

1 An _____ event is one which will probably never happen.
2 An object which cannot be moved is _____.
3 An _____ person gives no thanks for kindnesses received.
4 Another word for _____ is unlawful.
5 An _____ person is not responsible for his actions.
6 An _____ article is one you can do without.
7 The word _____ means unlucky.
8 A _____ person is rude and ill-mannered.

(C) Use these phrases in sentences of your own, but give the word in bold type an opposite meaning.

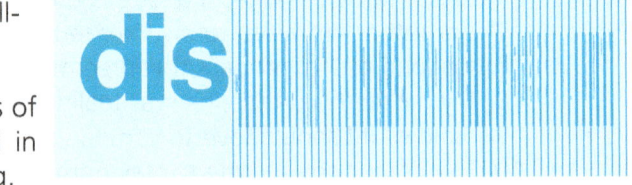

1 a **popular** man
2 **regular** attendance
3 an **efficient** worker
4 an **important** town
5 **favourable** weather
6 a **proper** remark

DIMINUTIVES

A diminutive is a word representing something small or something young.

Examples

kitten   a young cat
booklet   a small book

	Diminutive		Diminutive		Diminutive		Diminutive
bear	cub	eel	elver	horse	foal	stream	streamlet
cod	codling	elephant	calf	mare	filly	swan	cygnet
deer	fawn	frog	tadpole	owl	owlet	trout	fry
dog	puppy	goose	gosling	river	rivulet	whale	calf
eagle	eaglet	hare	leveret	sheep	lamb		

(A) Write one word for each of the following:

1 a young eel   **7** a baby owl   **13** a young whale
2 a baby goose   **8** a young horse   **14** a small river
3 a young elephant   **9** a young dog   **15** a young mare
4 a young sheep   **10** a young cod   **16** a young bear
5 a young hare   **11** a baby frog   **17** a baby eagle
6 a small stream   **12** a young deer   **18** a young swan

(B) Write the words which are missing from these sentences.

1 Several tiny _____ followed the eel up the river.
2 The mare and her _____ trotted round the paddock.
3 The _____ and her leverets lay down in the long grass.
4 The _____ and the foal were sold for £900.
5 The _____ and her lamb grazed in the field.
6 The elephant and her _____ walked slowly into the jungle clearing.
7 A swan and her two _____ floated majestically downstream.
8 The cat carried her _____ in her mouth.

THE ROYAL MINT

Hundreds of years ago coins were made in various towns in Britain, including Bristol, Canterbury, London, Winchester and York. After 1810 there was only one Royal Mint, that on Tower Hill, London, but in 1968a new mint was established at Llantrisant, South Wales, for the manufacture of Britain's decimal currency which was introduced on 15th February 1971.

The metal ingots from which coins are made are melted in closed crucibles, for about two hours, and the molten metal is then run into moulds to form coinage-bars which vary in width and thickness according to the coins that are to be made. These bars or strips are next passed between rollers to ensure that they are of uniform size and then put into machines which punch out the blank discs on which the design is to be stamped. After being examined to see that they are of the correct size and shape, these blank discs are fed into annealing drums which soften the metal in preparation for the stamping process. The design is stamped by powerful presses, both sides being done at the same time, and the finished coins are placed on a moving belt for inspection by overlookers who are trained to detect any faults. The newly-minted coins are tested for weight and, after being counted by an automatic machine, are placed in bags, sealed and stored in large strongrooms until required by the banks.

There are no silver coins in Britain's decimal currency, cupro-nickel being used for the 50p, 10p and 5p pieces.

A sealed bag of 50ppieces contains £250 worth, or 500 coins. Each bag of 10p pieces and 5p pieces contains £100 worth.

1 Name three towns at which coins were made hundreds of years ago.
2 After 1810 there was only one Royal Mint. Where was that?
3 Where was a new Royal Mint established in 1968?
4 When was Britain's decimal currency introduced?
5 How are metal ingots made into coinage-bars?
6 Why are these bars passed between rollers?
7 Why are the blank discs fed into annealing drums?
8 How are the finished coins counted?
9 What metal is used in place of silver for the decimal coins?
10 How many coins would there be in a bag of 5p pieces?

USING THE RIGHT PRONOUN

Mistakes are often made in the use of the pronouns **I** and **me**.

Which is correct?	Dad and **me** are going to the football match *or* Dad and **I** are going to the football match.
Make two sentences.	**a** Dad is going to the football match.
	b **I** am going to the football match.
	Me am going to the football match would be wrong.
So the correct sentence is	Dad and **I** are going to the football match.
Which is correct?	Uncle George sent a ticket for Dad and **me** *or* Uncle George sent a ticket for Dad and **I**.
Make two sentences.	**a** Uncle George sent a ticket for Dad.
	b Uncle George sent a ticket for **me**.
	Uncle George sent a ticket for I would be wrong.
So the correct sentence is	Uncle George sent a ticket for Dad and **me**.

After the word **between** always use the pronoun **me**.

Examples

*Between you and **I** he can't afford a new car.* (wrong)

*Between you and **me** he can't afford a new car.* (right)

Insert **I** or **me** to complete each sentence.

1 Pavana and _____ have won prizes in the drawing competition.
2 Prizes have been awarded to Pavana and _____.
3 Beth and _____ have been invited to Amy's party.
4 Amy has invited Beth and _____ to her party.
5 This is a secret between you and _____.
6 You and _____ must keep this matter secret.
7 The headmaster punished Ossie and _____ for being so late.
8 Ossie and _____ were punished by the headmaster for being so late.
9 Leroy and _____ are to share the sweets between us.
10 These sweets are to be shared between Leroy and _____.

ALPHABETICAL ORDER

Look at these words: **hea**r; **hea**p; **hea**t; **hea**d; **hea**l

Notice that the **first three letters** of each word are the same – **hea**.

To arrange these words in alpha-betical order, we must look at the **fourth** letter of each.

These are: **r p t d l**

Letters in alphabetical order: **d l p r t**

Words in alphabetical order: hea**d** hea**l** hea**p** hea**r** hea**t**

(A) Write the names of these objects in alphabetical order.

(B) Arrange each column of words in alphabetical order. Look at the **second** letter of each word.

1 signal   **2** physical   **3** chorus
    society   passport   crusade
    shudder   plumber   curfew
    student   portable   capsule
    skier   peculiar   climate

(C) Look at the **third** letter of each word when arranging them in alphabetical order.

1 blizzard   **2** ground   **3** splint
    blunder   granite   sparrow
    blockade   gruesome   sprawl
    bladder   grease   spectre
    bleak   gristle   spiral

(D) Arrange in alphabetical order, looking at the **fourth** letter.

1 catkin   **2** promise   **3** sprout   **4** retreat   **5** patriot   **6** assume
    cattle   profit   spruce   return   patch   assist
    catch   produce   sprint   retail   pattern   assets
    catalogue   problem   spray   retort   patent   assault
    catgut   proceed   spread   retire   patient   assorted

ADJECTIVES: FORMATION

Many adjectives are formed by adding **-ous** to a word.

Examples

*danger**ous*** *prosper**ous***
*pomp**ous*** *riot**ous***

Sometimes spelling changes are made when **-ous** is added.

1 Drop final **e**.
famous porous
ridiculous continuous

2 Change **y** to **i**.
furious injurious envious

3 Double the last letter.
marvellous libellous

4 Drop a letter.
humorous vigorous glamorous

5 Other changes.
cautious grievous miraculous

(A) Write the missing **adjectives**. When in difficulty consult your dictionary.

1 A substance which is full of pores is _____.
2 A person who has won fame is _____.
3 A person who envies others is _____.
4 A game which is played with vigour is _____.
5 A room in which there is plenty of space is _____.
6 A business which prospers is _____.
7 Berries which poison are _____.
8 An adventure in which there is peril is _____.
9 A person who behaves like a villain is _____.
10 A person who eats like a glutton is _____.

(B) Complete each sentence by using the **adjective** formed from the word in bold type.

1 The *Adventures of Tom Sawyer* is a _____ story. **humour**
2 The travellers gazed at the _____ scenery. **marvel**
3 The millionaire lives in a _____ house in France. **luxury**
4 The history of Britain is studded with _____ deeds. **glory**
5 When he heard of the retreat the general was _____ . **fury**
6 Paul has always been a _____ boy. **mischief**
7 Hosepipes were turned on the _____ crowd. **riot**
8 The show is _____ from 5.30 to 11 p.m. **continue**
9 Dense fog and smoke are _____ to health. **injury**
10 The crew of the trawler had a _____ escape from death. **miracle**.

Atropa Belladonna

POISONOUS

JOINING SENTENCES

You have learned in Book 3 how to join sentences by using **conjunctions**.

You can also join sentences by using **who**, **whom**, **that** and **which** (**relative pronouns**) and **whose** (**relative adjective**).

This is the lady.
She found your kitten.
*This is the lady **who** found your kitten.*

These are the trainers.
I like them best.
*These are the trainers **which** I like best.*
These are the trainers that I like best.

That is the man.
I saw him yesterday.
*That is the man **whom** I saw yesterday.*

The policeman spoke to the woman,
Her wallet had been stolen.
The policeman spoke to the woman
***whose** wallet had been stolen.*

(A) Use **who**, **whom**, **that**, **which** or **whose** to join each pair of sentences.

1 The police arrested the youth.
He had robbed the bank.
2 Mrs Baird gave Angela a bracelet.
It was made of gold.
3 The door was opened by a young girl.
She looked very unhappy.
4 This is the house.
Jack built it.
5 Sitting near us was a woman.
Her hair had been dyed blue.

(B) Use **who**, **whom**, **that**, **which** or **whose** to fill the gaps in these sentences.

1 Do you know anybody _____ first name beings with H?
2 Colin was the only pupil _____ was willing to help tidy up.
3 The prize _____ everyone wanted to win was the trip in a hot air balloon.
4 Anna is a friend _____ I have known all my life.
5 The canoe _____ was painted bright yellow was soon spotted by the helicopter crew.

SIMILES

When something is very **heavy** we say it is **as heavy as lead**.

This is because it is similar to lead in **weight**, although it may be quite different in other ways.

An expression of this kind is called a **simile**.

Examples:

as sweet as sugar	as busy as a bee	as dead as a doornail
as bold as brass	as clean as a new pin	as deafas a doorpost
as brave as a lion	as cool as a cucumber	as fit as a fiddle
as bright as a button		

(A) Write the missing words.

1 The old man was as _____ as a doorpost.
2 In walked James as _____ as brass.
3 Old Jacob Marley was as _____ as a doornail.
4 After a hot bath he was as _____ as a new pin.
5 Ann was as busy as a _____, helping Dad in the garden.
6 The full-back was as cool as a _____.
7 Every player in the team was as fit as a _____.
8 David got up at seven o'clock as bright as a _____.

When using similes, it is always best to use your own fresh, original ones.

This is one that a pupil made up:
*The twigs were stretched out **like a skinny hand**.*

(B) Complete these descriptions as vividly as you can.

1 James opened his exercise book with a heart as heavy as _____.
2 Sarah limped along the road like _____.
3 The princess's eyes were as blue as _____.
4 The ogre's breath smelt just like _____.
5 The headmaster's angry voice cut through the laughter like _____.

(C) Look again at the comparisons you have supplied in exercise **B** and explain why you think the similes are effective.

INSIDE THE VAULT

James sat down on the steps of the tomb and watched. The light ebbed from the church. Shadows began to pack the roof and crowd around the pillars and dark oak pews. The knight and his lady lay on their tomb with worn faces and stiff stone drapery. He was a crusading knight, armoured from head to pointed feet, his hands frozen in prayer; he must have known strange, hot, far-away places, and then come back to die in Ledsham, among elms and willows beside the Evenlode. James fetched himself a hassock to sit on that had been embroidered by the ladies of Ledsham Women's Institute, and thought about this, and other things, and listened to the tapping noises of Bert's pick and watched the dust and chippings fly up around the flagstone.

"I think this is the one," said Bert. "I reckon it is."

"What if someone comes?" said James.

"I'm seeing about the damp, aren't I?" said Bert. "Rising damp, they've got here. I don't know anything about any vault."

The church was very dark and quiet now, but not empty because no place that has been used for so long by so many people can ever be empty. Like all old buildings, it was full of their thoughts and feelings, and these thoughts and feelings seemed to crowd in upon James as he sat waiting and watching. He had asked Arnold to come, and Arnold had come at once and was there now, at James' elbow, waiting and watching with him.

"Here she comes," said Bert. He put his pick down and dug his fingers down under the edge of the flagstone. He heaved, muscles stood out like cords in his arms, the flagstone rocked, and tipped on to one side. James leaned forward.

"Hang on," said Bert, "I got to get through the next bit. I told you I mortared it up again." He swung the pick down: the floor split, mortar crumbled away downwards, and there was a jagged black hole, man-sized.

"There we are," said Bert. "Let's have that torch."

He pointed the torch down into the hole. "Want to have a look?"

James clutched the edge of the stone step. He said to Arnold, "Shall I?" and Arnold told him he'd be a silly idiot not to. He got up, rather slowly, and came forward, and lay down on his stomach and shone the torch down into the hole.

It was smaller than he'd expected. A little, crumbling underground room, with rough masonry walls and rubble all over the floor. And long stone boxes stacked up on top of each other: several at one side, one by itself on the other.

Bert's face appeared at the other side of the hole. "Let's have some light over here."

James swung the torch around. They could see the lettering now on top of the solitary box, black-shadowed in the beam of light. "I thought so," said Bert.

Here lyeth ye body of
Thomas Kempe Apothecarie
he departed this life ye last of October AD 1629
in the 63 yeare of his Age.

"Apothecary?" said James. His voice dropped into the vault, sounding deep and hollow.

"He couldn't go having them put sorcerer, could he?" said Bert. "Not if he wanted to be in here. The Church wouldn't hold with that."

"Why do you think he wanted to be there?" said James in a whisper. "He wasn't very religious, was he? Believing in all that magic, and hating priests."

The Ghost of Thomas Kempe   Penelope Lively

1 Why are the faces of the knight and his lady described as **worn**?
2 In what way are the knight's hands **frozen** in prayer?
3 What is a **hassock**?
4 How does Bert know that the flagstone he is trying to lift has been mortared in place?
5 Who is the first of the three to look into the vault?
6 Why is the small room very dark?
7 What are the long stone boxes?
8 On which side of the room is Thomas Kempe's box?
9 Give the day and month of Thomas Kempe's death.
10 In what century did Thomas Kempe die?
11 How old was he when he died?
12 What was his occupation as indicated on the box?
13 What was his true occupation?
14 Why could Thomas Kempe not have his true occupation shown on the box?
15 Say in what two ways he was not a religious man.

JOINING SENTENCES

You have already practised joining two sentences with conjunctions and relative pronouns.

It is possible to join together more than two sentences, and you can experiment with joining them in lots of different ways.

Roger likes English.
He likes maths.
He hates history.

*Roger likes English **and** maths **but** hates history.*

*Roger hates history **but** he likes English **and** maths.*

*Roger, **who** hates history, likes English **and** maths.*

***Although** Roger hates history, he likes English **and** maths.*

***While liking** English **and** maths, Roger hates history.*

*Roger, **who** likes English **and** maths, hates history.*

***Despite his hatred** of history, Roger likes English **and** maths.*

(A) Write one sentence in place of each group below.

1 The day was cold.
The day was windy.
It was only the first day of February.

2 The dog was barking.
He was trying to get over the gate.
The children kept away from him.

3 The office had closed.
The staff had departed.
It was not yet five o'clock.

4 I had intended to go for a walk.
It started to snow.

I sat by the fire.
I fell fast asleep.

5 Andrew had a bad leg.
He was unable to walk.
He stayed indoors with Gillian.
She read several stories to him.

6 We set off for the woods.
After a while there was a thunderstorm.
We had to shelter in an old barn.
It was close at hand.

(B) Combine each group of sentences below in two different ways.

1 Jake was frightened.
He was a nervous child.
His mother was late.

2 Work steadily.
Learn from your mistakes.
You will make progress.

3 The kitten was black.
The kitten was thin.
It was very hungry.
It had been abandoned.

USING THE RIGHT VERB

Learn how these verbs are used, then answer the questions.

to **accede** to a **request**	to **impose** a **fine**
to **avert** a **catastrophe**	to **inflict punishment**
to **contract** a **disease**	to **inherit** a **fortune**
to **contradict** a **statement**	to **interpret** a **foreign language**
to **denounce** an **impostor**	to **liberate** a **prisoner**
to **disperse** a **mob**	to **prophesy** the **future**
to **estimate** the **cost**	to **redeem** a **promise**
to **evade capture**	to **reveal** a **secret**
to **exterminate pests**	to **surmount** an **obstacle**
to **impart knowledge**	to **trespass** on **another's land**

(A) Copy and complete these phrases.

1 to _____ a secret
2 to _____ punishment
3 to _____ capture
4 to _____ knowledge
5 to _____ an obstacle
6 to _____ a prisoner
7 to _____ an impostor
8 to _____ the cost
9 to _____ a disease
10 to _____ on another's land

11 to interpret a _____
12 to inherit a _____
13 to disperse a _____
14 to accede to a _____
15 to prophesy the _____
16 to redeem a _____
17 to exterminate _____
18 to avert a _____
19 to contradict a _____
20 to impose a _____

(B) Write the verb which will complete each sentence correctly. Use the past tense where required.

1 On his father's death he will _____ a million pounds.
2 The magistrates _____ a fine of £50 and costs.
3 Mounted police were brought in to _____ the demonstrators.
4 The girl who _____ leukaemia is seriously ill.
5 A teacher should not only possess knowledge; he or she should know how to _____ it.
6 Simon _____ a dreadful accident by warning the police there was an obstacle on the railway track.
7 For nearly a month the escaped convict _____ capture.
8 The cost of building the new school is _____ at £6,000,000.

IDIOMS

In Book 3 you learnt ten sayings which are in common use.

Example   *to get into hot water*
            means to get into trouble

Expressions of this kind are called **idioms**.

Idiom	Meaning
tohave an axe togrind	to have something to gain by an action
tobe a wet blanket	to be a spoilsport
to draw the long bow	to exaggerate
tomake a clean breast of it	to confess to some wrong
totake the bull by the horns	to meet difficulties boldly
tobe under a cloud	to be under suspicion
tobe a dog in a manger	to deny to others what is useless to oneself
toshow the white feather	to show cowardice
tobury the hatchet	to settle a quarrel and live in peace
to flog a dead horse	to do work which produces no results

(A) Complete these **idioms** and describe a situation where each could apply.

1 to be under a _____
2 to flog a _____ horse
3 to be a dog in a _____
4 to draw the _____ _____
5 to bury the _____

6 to have an axe _____ _____
7 to take the bull _____ _____ _____
8 to be a wet _____
9 to make a clean _____ _____ _____
10 to show the white _____

(B) Rewrite these sentences, substituting the **idiom** for the words in bold type.

1 The detective was determined to **meet the difficulties boldly**.
2 Jamie told his uncle not to be a **spoilsport**.
3 The old rivals will soon **settle their quarrel and live in peace**.
4 The prefect was **under suspicion** at school.
5 The old sailor is very fond of **exaggerating**.

SYNONYMS: SIMILARS

	Synonym		Synonym		Synonym
abrupt	sudden	diminutive	small	loathe	hate
accommodation	room	disperse	scatter	melancholy	sad
altitude	height	eminent	famous	odour	smell
amiable	friendly	endeavour	try	penetrate	pierce
briefshort	interior	inside	prohibited forbidden	f	
comprehend	understand	intoxicated	drunk	reluctant	unwilling
demonstrate	show	invincible	unbeatable		

(A) Write a simpler word in place of each word in bold type.

1 Smoking in the factory is **prohibited**.
2 The **odour** of fried sausages came from the kitchen.
3 I read a **brief** report of the accident.
4 We failed to obtain **accommodation** at the hotel.
5 This year our cricket team has proved **invincible**.
6 He was most **reluctant** to leave home.
7 We will **endeavour** to deliver the goods today.
8 Mounted police were sent to **disperse** the large crowd.
9 The plane was flying at an **altitude** of 10,000 metres.
10 Our train came to an **abrupt** stop.

(B) In each group below select the word which is similar in meaning to the word in bold type.

1 **eminent**
handsome
skilful
famous

5 **intoxicated**
drunk
unconscious
sober

9 **comprehend**
fear
understand
pretend

2 **loathe**
hate
adore
respect

6 **demonstrate**
fight
squander
show

10 **interior**
cheap
inside
common

3 **amiable**
rude
stout
friendly

7 **melancholy**
sad
jolly
greedy

11 **penetrate**
thicken
pierce
collapse

4 **diminutive**
tough
dark
small

8 **abrupt**
sudden
brief
rough

12 **odour**
dislike
heavy
smell

A PONY FOR JODY

Jody could begin to see things now. He looked into the box stall and then stepped back quickly.

A red pony colt was looking at him out of the stall. Its tense ears were forward and a light of disobedience was in its eyes. Its coat was rough and thick as an Airedale's fur and its mane was long and tangled. Jody's throat collapsed in on itself and cut his breath short.

"He needs a good currying," his father said, "and if I ever hear of you not feeding him or leaving his stall dirty I'll sell him off in a minute."

Jody couldn't bear to look at the pony's eyes any more. He gazed down at his hands for a moment, and he asked very shyly: "Mine?" No one answered him. He put his hand out toward the pony. Its grey nose came close, sniffing loudly, and then the lips drew back and the strong teeth closed on Jody's fingers. The pony shook its head up and down and seemed to laugh with amusement. Jody regarded his bruised fingers. "Well," he said with pride – "well, I guess he can bite all right." The two men laughed, somewhat in relief. Carl Tiffin went out of the barn and walked up a side-hill to be by himself, for he was embarrassed, but Billy Buck stayed. It was easier to talk to Billy Buck. Jody asked again – "Mine?"

Billy became professional in tone. "Sure! That is, if you look out for him and break him right. I'll show you how. He's just a colt. You can't ride him for some time."

The Red Pony John Steinbeck

1 Why did Jody step back from the box stall?
2 Which two words indicate the pony's mood and attitude?
3 Why did Jody's throat "collapse in on Itself"?
4 What is another word for **currying**?
5 What two things did Jody's father warn him he must do?
6 Why couldn't he bear to look at the pony's eyes any more?
7 How did Jody bruise his fingers?
8 Why did Jody speak of the pony with pride?
9 Why were the two men relieved as they laughed?
10 Why did Carl Tiflin want to be by himself?
11 Why could the pony not be ridden for some time?
12 Who was going to help Jody break in the pony?

SILENT LETTERS

Some words can be difficult to spell because they contain silent letters.

Learn the words in these lists and then answer the questions in exercise A.

silent c	silent h	silent p	silent t
ascend	exhausted	cupboard	castle
crescent	ghost	pneumatic	christen
muscle	honest	pneumonia	fasten
scenery	rhubarb	psalm	listen
scent	rhyme	psychology	mistletoe
science	shepherd	raspberry	moisten
scissors	vehicle	receipt	whistle

(A) Fill each space with the missing silent letter. Refer to the lists on the above.

1 tired out
ex _ austed

2 a curving road
cres _ ent

3 a sacred song
_ salm

4 to make slightly damp
mois _ en

5 a person who looks after sheep
shep _ erd

6 inflammation of the lungs
_ neumonia

(B) Use your dictionary to help you find these words.

1 an extinct winged reptile
pte _ _ _ _ _ _ _

2 mixed; of all sorts
mis _ _ _ _ _ _ _ _ _

3 sum of money borrowed to buy
a house **mor _ _ _ _ _**

4 colour of army uniforms kha _ _

5 a pen-name; assumed name
pse _ _ _ _ _ _

6 amazed and horrified **agh _ _ _**

7 person entitled to inherit **he _ _**

8 small boat **din _ _ _**

9 an evergreen shrub with large flowers
rho _ _ _ _ _ _ _ _ _

10 a bird of the grouse family
pta _ _ _ _ _ _

SENTENCE STRUCTURE

Let me know when you are ready.

When you are ready let me know.

Both these sentences contain exactly the same words, although not in the same order.

*A rattlesnake **bit** the lumberjack.*

*The lumberjack **was bitten** by a rattlesnake.*

Both these sentences convey the same idea, but the words they contain are not exactly the same.

(**a**) contains the word **bit**, the **past tense** of bite.

(**b**) contains the word **bitten**, the **past participle** of bite.

(**A**) Rewrite each sentence below, using the same words, but commencing with the word in bold type.

  1 Julia persisted in talking **although** she had been warned not to do so.
  2 She ordered the dress **without** thinking how she could pay for it.
  3 Two sailors were having an argument **on** the quay.
  4 The convict was recaptured **just** as night was falling.
  5 The express train rushed into the tunnel **with** a shriek of its whistle.
  6 You will be seriously ill **if** you do not check that cough.
  7 A huge log fire blazed **in** the great hall of the castle.
  8 The girl was up and about **long** before daybreak.

(**B**) Rewrite these sentences, beginning with the word in bold type in each case, and making such changes as are necessary.

  1 Charles Dickens wrote **A** *Christmas Carol.*
  2 The Rovers beat **the** Wanderers 2-0 last Saturday.
  3 A gang of thieves stole **the** valuable portrait.
  4 The County Architect drew **the** plans of the dining-hall.
  5 The heavy fall shook **the** frail old gentleman.
  6 The twins took **Spot** to the park.
  7 Our puppy tore **that** curtain.
  8 The three girls chose **the** curtains for the lounge.
  9 The one-eyed parrot had eaten **every** single chocolate.
  10 Penelope Lively wrote ***The** Ghost ofThomas Kempe.*

ALPHABETICAL ORDER

(A) Arrange the words in each group in alphabetical order. Look at the **fifth** letter of each word.

1 straw
strap
straight
stray
strand

2 fortress
fortunate
fortify
forth
fortnight

3 handicap
handy
handsome
handle
handful

4 partner
partly
partake
party
partial

5 catapult
catastrophe
catalogue
catacomb
cataract

6 compile
complain
compel
compose
compare

This is a drawing of a ten-volume encyclopaedia. Each volume is numbered and also shows the first four letters of the first word and the last word it contains.

(B) Give the numbers of the volumes in which you would look for the following words.

1 longitude
2 Dunlop
3 meteor
4 indigo
5 cardinal
6 balsa
7 tambourine

8 athletics
9 portcullis
10 Henry VIII
11 Kiel Canal
12 gannet
13 vodka
14 Jolly Roger

15 foundry
16 decimal
17 resin
18 Napoleon
19 shorthand
20 crypt

ADJECTIVES: FORMATION

Noun	Adjective	Noun	Adjective
athlete	athletic	influence	influential
benefit	beneficial	metal	metallic
circle	circular	method	methodical
credit	creditable	muscle	muscular
custom	customary	nonsense	nonsensical
effect	effective	picture	picturesque
energy	energetic	science	scientific
fire	fiery	skill	skilful
fraud	fraudulent	sympathy	sympathetic
giant	gigantic	system	systematic

(A) Form **adjectives** from these nouns.

1 muscle	7 skill	13 science
2 effect	8 benefit	14 fire
3 fraud	9 system	15 picture
4 athlete	10 credit	16 influence
5 sympathy	11 method	17 circle
6 energy	12 giant	18 metal

(B) Write the missing **adjectives**.

1 an _____ remedy   **effect**
2 a _____ craftsman   **skill**
3 a _____ sound   **metal**
4 an _____ man   **athlete**
5 a _____ age   **science**
6 a _____ saw   **circle**
7 an _____ worker   **energy**   10 a _____ friend   **sympathy**
8 a _____ holiday   **benefit**   11 a _____ scene   **picture**
9 a _____ reply   **nonsense**   12 a _____ scheme   **fraud**

(C) Complete each sentence by inserting the **adjective** formed from the noun in bold type.

1 Police made a _____ search of the building.   **system**
2 The scientist is noted for his _____ work.   **method**
3 Paul's success was a most _____ achievement.   **credit**
4 The key was not in its _____ place.   **custom**
5 We stayed at a _____ Cornish fishing village.   **picture**

CAPITAL LETTERS

Capital letters are used for:

names of persons	geographical names
pets	nations
days	languages
months *but not seasons*	titles of books, poems, songs, etc.
special holidays	

(A) Rewrite these sentences, using capital letters where necessary.

1 the river thames is sometimes referred to as old father thames.
2 both german and italian are taught at grosvenor grammar school.
3 rudyard kipling, who was born in india, wrote many fine books, the most famous being the jungle book.
4 easter is a movable festival which may come in march or april, but christmas is not.
5 the bank of england is sometimes called the old lady of threadneedle street.
6 linda's brother colin is a patient at the middlesex hospital.
7 the white tower in the tower of london was built by gundulf, bishop of rochester, about A.D. 1078.
8 from monday to friday the shop closes at 5.30; on saturdays it closes at 1 o'clock.

(B) Some punctuation marks are missing from the sentences below. Write out the sentences correctly punctuated.

1 Would you like to tour Europe and see its wonderful sights
2 In the market there were ample supplies of apples pears oranges bananas peaches and grapes
3 James did you give my message to the headmaster asked his mother
4 Yes Mum I gave it to him before lessons began replied James
5 Some members wont be present but it doesnt matter
6 The ticket bore the date Thurs 26th Sept in bold type
7 The bat we played with was Toms but the ball was Duncans
8 Oh dear exclaimed Miss Taylor in alarm I have lost my purse

ENCOUNTER WITH A DINOSAUR

Something was swimming toward the lighthouse tower.

It was a cold night, as I have said; the high tower was cold, the light coming and going and the Fog Horn calling and calling through the ravelling mist. You couldn't see far and you couldn't see plain, but there was the deep sea moving on its way about the night earth, flat and quiet, the colour of grey mud, and here were the two of us alone in the high tower, and there, far out at first, was a ripple, followed by a wave, a rising, a bubble, a bit of froth. And then, from the surface of the cold sea came a head, a large head, dark-coloured, with immense eyes, and then a neck. And then – not a body – but more neck and more! The head rose a full forty feet above the water on a slender and beautiful dark neck. Only then did the body, like a little island of black coral and shells and crayfish, drip up from the subterranean. There was a flicker of tail. In all, from head to tail, I estimated the monster at ninety or a hundred feet.

I don't know what I said. I said something.

"Steady, boy, steady," whispered McDunn.

"It's impossible!" I said.

"No, Johnny, *we're* impossible. *It's* like it always was ten million years ago. It hasn't changed. It's *us* and the land that've changed, become impossible. *Us!*"

It swam slowly and with a great dark majesty out in the icy waters, far away. The fog came and went about it, momentarily erasing its shape.

The Fog Horn Ray Bradbury

 1 Where were the men standing?
 2 What sound could be heard?
 3 How much visibility was there?
 4 Which movement first told the men there was something in the sea?
 5 Where did the men first see this movement?
 6 At what height above the water did the head rise?
 7 To what does the writer compare the monster's body?
 8 How long was the monster?
 9 When did McDunn suggest these monsters had once lived?
10 Why was the monster not continuously visible?

HOMOPHONES

herd	a number of animals together	**profit**	gain; benefit
heard	past tense of hear	**prophet**	one who foretells events
key	locks a door, etc.	**sew**	to work with needle and thread
quay	a landing-place for ships	**sow**	to scatter seed
night	time between evening and morning	**stile**	steps in a fence or wall
knight	a titled gentleman	**style**	fashion
muscle	part of the body	**vale**	a valley
mussel	a shellfish	**veil**	thin material covering face
place	a particular part of space	**stationery**	writing materials
plaice	a flat-fish	**stationary**	standing still

(A) Choose the correct word from the pair above to complete each sentence.

1 vale   veil
The bride wore a _____ of lace.

2 stationery   stationary
The fast sports car collided with a _____ saloon car.

3 profit   prophet
The _____ foretold the defeat of the Hebrews.

4 sow   sew
In spring farmers plough their fields and _____ the seed.

5 muscle   mussel
Having pulled a _____ in his thigh the centre-half had to leave the field.

(B) Complete each sentence by using a suitable pair of homophones from your list.

1 The thundering hoofs of the stampeding _____ of buffalo could be _____ from a long way off.

2 The _____ to the sailor's chest was found lying on the _____.

3 The black _____ rode out one _____ to attack the baron's castle.

4 The athlete vaulted over the _____ in fine _____.

5 The fishmonger put the huge _____ in a prominent _____ on the marble slab.

FIVE FAMILIAR USES OF THE COMMA

1 Commas are used with terms of address.

"Marva, come here!"
"Yes, sir."
"I think, your majesty, we are lost."

2 Commas are used in lists.

We bought cakes, crisps, sweets and lemonade.

3 Commas are used to separate words and phrases like **oh**, **well**, **yes**, **as a matter of fact**, at the beginning of a sentence.

Well, I did warn you.

4 Commas are used to separate words like **please** at the end of a sentence.

Can you help me, please?

5 Commas are used in the punctuation of direct speech.

Robert said, "It is getting late."
"It is getting late," said Robert.
"It is getting late," said Robert, "and we should be leaving."

Copy these sentences, adding commas where they are needed.

1 "Your highness your crown is crooked."
2 I have packed sweaters socks and anoraks.
3 "Jake can you hear me?"
4 "Can I help you madam?"
5 "Yes I want to buy a warm vest."
6 I've brushed the stairs I've polished the furniture I've cleaned the windows and now I'm going to have a rest.
7 "Good morning Mrs Brown."
8 David asked "Are you awake?"
9 "I'm fast asleep" replied Tom quietly.
10 "I know very well" said David "that you're wide awake."
11 "Anna and Matthew it's time for bed."
12 Uncle Fred can speak German French Spanish Italian and Russian.
13 As a matter of fact you are right.
14 "Will you lock the door after you please?"
15 "Hello James."

RHYMES

farms	floors	roars	I	see	doors	me	flour
be	rye	tower	arms	devour	sails	flails	

Ⓐ Write the words, numbered 1 to 15, which fill the spaces in the verses below. The poem is about a windmill on a farm.

Behold! a giant am _____   **1**
Aloft here in my _____.   **2**
With my granite jaws I _____   **3**
The maize, and the wheat and the _____,   **4**
And grind them into _____.   **5**

I look down over the _____   **6**
In the fields of grain I _____   **7**
The harvest that is to _____,   **8**
And I fling to the air my _____   **9**
For I know it is all for _____.   **10**

I hear the sound of _____   **11**
Far off, from the threshing _____,   **12**
In barns, with their open _____,   **13**
And the wind, the wind in my _____   **14**
Louder and louder _____.   **15**

Ⓑ Write the word needed to complete each sentence. In each case the missing word rhymes with the word in bold type.

1 He was sorry to have to _____ the invitation.   **fine**
2 She will _____ her hundredth birthday tomorrow.   **wait**
3 The architect will _____ the site for the school.   **play**
4 The rabbit was caught in a _____.   **pair**
5 The _____ against smoking will receive strong support.   **main**
6 Wise parents rarely _____ in the quarrels of their children.   **deer**
7 When you pay a bill you should obtain a _____.   **meet**
8 _____ furniture is very old and often very valuable.   **beak**
9 We are going to _____ our parts for the school play.   **purse**
10 The tourists stayed at a _____ village in the Alps.   **desk**

PREPOSITIONS

The words **in**, **under** and **on** show how the word 'dog' is related to the words **car**, **table** and **chair**.

A word which shows the relationship between a noun (or pronoun) and some other word in a sentence is called a preposition.

above	*against*	*at*	*beneath*	*from*	*off*	*over*	*up*
across	*along*	*before*	*by*	*near*	*on*	*through*	
after	*around*	*below*	*for*	*of*	*outside*	*under*	

The dog is **on** the chair.

The dog is **under** the table.

The dog is **in** the car.

(A) Insert the prepositions in the list on the above in their correct places in the sentences which follow.

1 Judith is suffering _____ appendicitis.
2 Crowds of people strolled _____ the promenade.
3 Grandpa was seated _____ a blazing fire.
4 Henry leaned _____ the wall of the gymnasium.
5 The dog ran _____ the cat, but could not catch it.
6 Drake was the first Englishman to sail _____ the world.
7 The dog jumped right _____ the hollyhocks.
8 A long queue formed _____ the football ground.
9 Lovely water lilies floated _____ the surface of the pond.
10 A workman fell _____ a ladder and was badly hurt.

Using prepositions correctly

between	Things are shared between two persons.
among	Things are shared among more than two.
in	Shows position in one place. *e.g.* The budgie was in its cage.

into	Shows movement from one place to another. *e.g.* The budgie hopped from the table into its cage.
differ	The twins differ **from** each other in some ways. I beg to differ **with** you on that point.
different	This book is quite different **from** the one I read last. (Never use **to** or **than** with different.)
beside	Means by the side of. *e.g.* Simon sits beside me in school.
besides	Means in addition to. *e.g.* Another bicycle was stolen besides John's.

Note that the same word may be followed by different prepositions.

Examples	a	*I agree **with** you in everything you say.* *I hope you will agree **to** my suggestion.*
	b	*The headmaster was angry **with** the children.* *He was angry **at** their bad behaviour.*
	c	*The soldier died **for** his country.* *The soldier died **of** wounds.*
	d	*The traveller lives **in** Bournemouth.* *He lives **at** 27 Broad Street.*
	e	*He would not part **with** a penny.* *She hates to part **from** her mother.*

(B) Use a **preposition** to complete each sentence.

1 The children were walking about _____ the classroom.
2 The children went from the playground _____ the classroom.
3 Do you agree _____ this proposal?
4 He will agree _____ everything you say.
5 The prize was divided _____ the two winners.
6 The prize was divided _____ several competitors.
7 Angus now lives _____ Edinburgh.
8 He lives with his aunt _____ 49 Argyll Street.
9 The matron stood _____ the patient's bed.
10 He has a private income _____ his large salary.

(C) Use these phrases in sentences of your own.

1 walked in   **3** walked on   **5** walked behind
2 walked into   **4** walked across   **6** walked under

TARKA FIGHTS DEADLOCK

Between boulders and rocks crusted with shellfish and shaggy with seaweed, past worm-channelled posts that marked the fairway for fishing boats at high water, the pack hunted the otter. Off each post a gull launched itself, cackling angrily as it looked down at the animals. Tarka reached the sea. He walked slowly into the surge of a wavelet, and sank away from the chop of old Harper's jaws, just as Deadlock ran through the pack. Hounds swam beyond the line of waves, while people stood at the sea-lap and watched the huntsman wading to his waist. It was said that the otter was dead-beat, and probably floating stiffly in the shallow water. After a few minutes the huntsman shook his head, and withdrew the horn from his waistcoat. He filled his lungs and stopped his breath and was tightening his lips for the four long notes of the call-off, when a brown head with hard dark eyes was thrust out of the water a yard from Deadlock. Tarka stared into the hound's face and cried "Ic-yang".

The head sank. Swimming under Deadlock, Tarka bit on to the loose skin of the flews and pulled the hound's head under the water. Deadlock tried to twist round and crush the otter's skull in his jaws, but he struggled vainly. Bubbles blew out of his mouth. Soon he was choking. The hounds did not know what was happening. Deadlock's hindlegs kicked the air weakly. The huntsman waded out and pulled him inshore, but Tarka loosened his bite only when he needed new air in his lungs.

Tarka the Otter   Henry Williamson

1 Name three physical features that were part of the shore where the otter was hunted.
2 What made the gulls angry?
3 What were the people standing on the shore doing?
4 What did people think had happened to Tarka?
5 Why did the huntsman shake his head?
6 What did he then prepare to do?
7 What prevented him from performing this action?
8 Why was Deadlock's struggle in vain?
9 What part of Deadlock's body was above the surface of the water?
10 Why did Tarka loosen his bite?
11 Which word in the passage means "navigable channel"?
12 Which word means "the hanging lips of a bloodhound"?

CONTAINERS

A **caddy** is a container for **tea**.

A **purse** is a container for **money**.

barrel	holster	rucksack	sheath
caddy	kitbag	safe	toolbox
chest	manger	satchel	vase
crate	purse	scabbard	wallet
cupboard	quiver	scuttle	wardrobe
dustbin			

(A) Write the names of the containers shown in the pictures.

(B) Write in order the words which have been omitted from these sentences.

   1 The carpenter's tools were kept in a large wooden _____.
   2 The china was packed in straw in a large _____.
   3 Penelope poured the contents of two packets of tea into the _____.
   4 There are piles of plates in the kitchen _____.
   5 Sarah hung her best dress in her mother's _____.
   6 The cowboy put his revolver back in its _____.
   7 The archer took an arrow from his _____.
   8 Many walkers carry a _____ on their backs.
   9 The _____ in Black Beauty's stable was piled up with hay.
 10 Farmer Giles gave the haymakers a _____ of cider.

WORDS WITH MORE THAN ONE MEANING

Some words have more than one meaning.
*You should **check** the working ofevery sum .*
*The bookmaker wore a **check** suit.*

charge	*coach*	*ground*	*plane*	*stern*
chest	*express*	*litter*	*spring*	*temple*

(A) Write the numbers from 1 to 10 in a column, then opposite each write the word which will complete both sentences.

1 The beach was covered with _____ after the vast crowd of holiday-makers had left.
Trixie had a _____ of six lovely puppies.

2 The pirates kept the treasure in a wooden _____.
A cold on the _____ often makes breathing difficult.

3 The _____ for admission to the circus was £5.
The troops were ordered to _____ the enemy.

4 He could not find words to _____ his thanks.
The _____ train was travelling at 200 kilometres an hour.

5 The _____ was covered with fallen leaves.
The coffee was _____ by machinery.

6 The daffodil is my favourite _____ flower.
The _____ of the clock was broken.

7 A _____ man is very strict and severe.
The _____ of a ship is the rear part.

8 Carpenters _____ wood to make it smooth.
The _____ circled the airport twice before landing.

9 Several people were worshipping in the _____.
A blow on the _____ rendered the man unconscious.

10 A new teacher had been appointed to _____ the boys at cricket.
The _____ was carrying thirty-five passengers on a school journey.

11 . 12

(B) Show how these words can have more than one meaning.

1 fly	**3** plain	**5** bank	**7** train	**9** rule	**11** sink
2 drop	**4** present	**6** wave	**8** punch	**10** board	**12** pen

OCCUPATIONS

actress	conjurer	messenger	sculptor
artist	engineer	optician	solicitor
ballerina	fishmonger	photographer	surgeon
beautician	interpreter	physiotherapist	taxidermist
caddie	juggler	pilot	teacher
chauffeur	lumberjack	reporter	ventriloquist
chiropodist	mechanic		

(A) Write the names of these occupations from the list above.

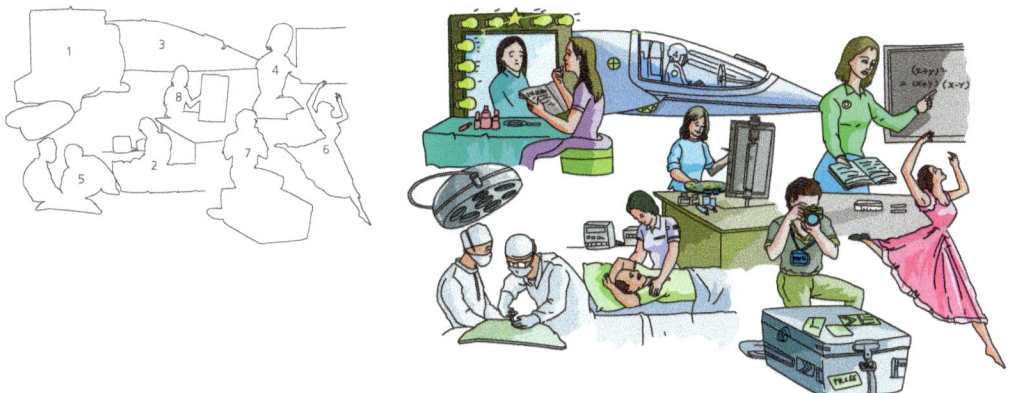

(B) Choose the word in the list which will complete each of these sentences correctly.

1 When the _____ had finished stuffing and mounting the barn owl it looked very lifelike.

2 People who travel in foreign countries often need an _____ to make themselves understood.

3 An exhibition of paintings by a local _____ was held in the town hall.

4 She is a trained _____ specializing in skin care.

5 The _____ was forced to make a crash landing.

6 A number of experienced _____ were consulted about the new bridge.

7 The _____ told the magistrates that her client had been assaulted by the defendant.

8 The _____ collected the tickets at the booking office.

9 He has arthritis and is treated by a _____ each week.

10 The _____ performed the heart transplant successfully.

ANTONYMS: OPPOSITES

	Opposite		Opposite		Opposite
ancient	modern	exterior	interior	present	absent
ascend	descend	famine	glut	punishment	reward
assemble	disperse	friend	enemy	question	answer
attack	defence	frugal	extravagant	retreat	advance
captivity	freedom	happiness	misery	sweet	sour
cautious	reckless	import	export	transpare	opaque
coarse	fine	increase	decrease	vacant	occupied
compulsory	voluntary	inferior	superior	vague	precise
defeat	victory	junior	senior	wax	wane
deny	admit	majority	minority	weak	strong
entrance	exit	maximum	minimum		
expand	contract	permanent	temporary		

(A) What are the **opposites** of the following words?

1 expand	**6** increase	**11** entrance	**15** import
2 victory	**7** punishment	**12** transparent	**16** permanent
3 maximum	**8** majority	**13** cautious	**17** exterior
4 famine	**9** captivity	**14** descend	**18** compulsory
5 coarse	**10** inferior		

(B) Copy and complete each sentence by inserting the **opposite** of the word in bold type.

1 Both the _____ and the **exit** of the building were well lit.
2 This file is too _____; try a **fine** one.
3 During his long service the general had known both _____ and **defeat**.
4 Service with the Armed Forces was _____ for men and **voluntary** for women.
5 The castle is an _____ building, but the church is quite **modern**.
6 The _____ of the house needs painting but the **interior** is perfect.
7 The team is strong in _____ but weak in **defence**.
8 **Cautious** motorists often have to suffer for the folly of the _____.
9 After two years of _____ the prisoners of war thought **freedom** was wonderful.
10 The teacher believed in _____ for the wicked and **reward** for the good.
11 England _____ more goods than it **exports**.
12 **Vague** answers will not do; I need _____ information.

HYPHENS

Hyphens join some compound adjectives.	**Hyphens can indicate that a word continues on the next line.**
twenty-eight	*Sam is always exag-gerating*
happy-go-lucky	It's best NOT to split words if you can avoid it.
Hyphens join some compound nouns.	Always divide the word at a sensible point between syllables.
horse-box *make-up*	The hyphen at the end of a line indicates the word is about to be split. You DON'T need a hyphen on the next line as well.

(A) Use hyphens to join the compound adjectives.

1 long lost relation   **4** old fashioned clothes
2 grey green eyes   **5** sixty five candles
3 fifty minute tests

(B) Which compound noun in each trio is correctly punctuated?
Use your dictionary for reference.

1 body building	body-building	bodybuilding
2 cup board	cup-board	cupboard
3 merry go round	merry-go-round	merrygoround
4 public house	public-house	publichouse
5 lay by	lay-by	layby

(C) Which word break is acceptable?

| **1** ridiculo-
us | r-
idicueous | ridicu-
lous |
| **2** examina-
tion | examinat-
ion | |

(D) Use your dictionary to find three examples of compound nouns which have hyphens.

PARAGRAPH TOPICS AND SEQUENCING

A **paragraph** is a series of sentences about **thesametopic** .

Example

If you want to make successful cakes, just remember four simple rules. Firstly, always weigh and measure the ingredients. Secondly, use the right size cake tin. Thirdly, set the oven on the recommended setting. Lastly, wait patiently until the cake is cooked.

Planning a composition means choosing the topics for the paragraphs and arranging them in a sensible order.

(A) What is the topic of each of these paragraphs?

1 Don't leave everything to the last minute. A project needs careful researching, careful planning and careful presentation. All this takes time and no stage can be left out.

2 My grandfather was a lonely man in many ways, especially after Grandma died. He had few hobbies and found it difficult to make friends. Fortunately, he had his two dogs Gipsy and Rusty, who went everywhere with him. He was 92 when he died. I still miss him.

(B) Arrange these topics in a sensible order.

1 Thebirthday party
a Saying goodbye to everyone
b Blowing out the candles
c Sending out the invitations
d Opening the door as everyone arrives
e Laying the table

2 A typical Saturday
a Watching television until bedtime
b Unpacking the carrier bags
c Shopping with my mother
d Helping to cook supper
e Tidying my bedroom before breakfast

(C) **Plan** a composition on a class outing. List your paragraph topics in order.

(D) Choose three of the topics below and write one paragraph about each.

a A great football match
b Your best friend
c Your favourite meal
d Your favourite place
e A bad day

AGREEMENT OF SUBJECT AND VERB

The **subject** of a sentence must agree with its **verb** in number.

A **singular subject** requires a **singular verb**.

A **plural subject** requires a **plural verb**.

Example
Cows are *very useful animals.*

Now look carefully at this sentence.

*A fine **selection** ofused cars **was** on view.*

The noun **selection**, which is the **subject**, is **singular**, so the singular verb **was** must be used.

Always use a **singular verb** with **each, anybody, nobody, everybody, everyone, no one, either, neither**.

Example
Neither *ofthese knives* **is** *very sharp.*

(A) Choose the correct **verb** from the pair above to complete each sentence.

1 has   have
A violet _____ a fragrant smell.

2 has   have
Violets _____ a fragrant smell.

3 wasn't   weren't
The book _____ on the shelf.

4 wasn't   weren't
The books _____ on the shelf.

5 tries   try
The boys _____ hard to make good progress.

6 tries   try
The boy _____ hard to make good progress.

(B) Watch for the **subject** in each sentence and use the verb which agrees with it in number.

1 has   have
One of the twins _____ very red hair.

2 has   have
Both of the twins _____ rosy cheeks.

3 was   were
The bunch of keys _____ lost in the street.

4 was   were
The keys _____ lost in the street.

5 makes   make
A box of chocolates _____ a nice present.

6 makes   make
Chocolates _____ a nice present.

7 is   are
Road accidents _____ increasing in number.

8 is   are
The number of Road accidents _____ increasing.

METAPHORS

Both similes and metaphors describe by making comparisons.

*Michael ran down the road **as fast as a hare**.* (Simile)

*Michael **hared** down the road.* (Metaphor)

A simile explains the comparison and begins with **like, as, as if** or **as though**.

A metaphor hints at the comparison and leaves you to work it out for yourself.

Examples of metaphors

*Anna **flew** downstairs.*

What two things are being compared?
Anna and a bird.
How is Anna like a bird?
They both move quickly.

*My father **towered** over us.*
What two things are being compared?
My father and a tower.
How is my father like a tower?
They are both very tall.

(A) Each of these sentences contains a metaphor. Explain what is being compared in each, and how the two things are alike.

1 The clouds sailed across the sky.
2 We ducked down out of sight.
3 Jo just skimmed quickly through the book.
4 Matthew wolfed down his lunch in three minutes.
5 My father just exploded when I told him the news.

(B) Describe a situation where these metaphorical expressions could be used.

1 striking while the iron is hot
2 getting into hot water
3 turning over a new leaf
4 sitting on the fence
5 letting the cat out the bag

WORDS WHICH SAVE WORK

One word can sometimes do the work of several.

Example

People who eat more than is good for them *are rarely healthy.*

Gluttons are rarely healthy.

accidentally	immediately	revolved
apologized	librarian	speechless
author	occasionally	surrendered
drought	postponed	survivors
fearlessly	recently	talkative

(A) In each sentence below, replace the words in bold type with a labour-saving word from the list above.

1 I met Robert in London **not long ago**.
2 The rebel leader **gavehimsdf up** to the Government forces.
3 Owing to bad weather the school sports had to be **put off to a later date**.
4 Gillian is a bright pupil but rather **fond of talking too much**.
5 After his surprise win Roger was **incapableof speaking** .
6 It is wise to visit the dentist **every now and then**.
7 The **great shortage of rain** has ruined the crops.
8 Of the forty-two passengers in the plane crash, there were only three **who remained alive**.

(B) Use the remaining words from the list to replace these words in bold type.

1 The window was broken **by accident**.
2 The hooligans were ordered to leave the cinema **without further delay**.
3 I received a copy of the book of poems from the **man who wroteit** .
4 The policeman tackled the armed robber **without any fear**.
5 Robert asked the **man in chargeof thelibrary** if he could recommend the book he had chosen.
6 The chairman of the meeting **expressed his regret** for his late arrival.
7 The blades of the electric fan **turned round and round** at a fantastic speed.

HOMOPHONES

bail	**a** money paid to set a person free **b** crosspiece of a wicket	**lessen**	to grow or make less
		lesson	something learnt or taught
bale	a large bundle	**root**	underground part of a plant
		route	a way to go; a road
berth	place to sleep on a ship	**sight**	power or act of seeing
birth	being born	**site**	position or place
faint	**a** condition like sleep or death **b** weak, not plain	**soar**	to fly upwards or at a great height
feint	a sham blow or attack	**sore**	painful
gilt	thin covering of gold	**hoard**	to save and store up
guilt	state of having done wrong	**horde**	a crowd, e.g. of hooligans
stake	a pointed stick		
steak	a slice of meat or fish		

From the list of the left, choose the correct homophone to complete each sentence.

1 We watched the skylark _____ up into the sky.
2 The champion made a _____ with his left then landed with a punishing right hook.
3 Two of the accused men were released on _____.
4 Our new house is being built on a sunny _____.
5 On the voyage to America Tony slept on an upper _____.
6 The prisoner admitted his _____ and was sentenced to three months' imprisonment.
7 No sooner had he scored a goal than he was surrounded by a _____ of hooligans.
8 A strong _____ was driven into the earth to support the young apple tree.
9 The tablets he took did much to _____ the pain in his chest.
10 Before we began our tour, Dad planned the _____ we were to take.

CREATURE NOISES

Animal	Noise	Animal	Noise	Animal	Noise
apes	gibber	horses	neigh	oxen	low
bears	growl	hounds	bay	parrots	screech; talk
bulls	bellow	hyenas	laugh; scream	rabbits	squeal
crows	caw	lambs	bleat	snakes	hiss
donkeys	bray	mice	squeak	sparrows	chirp
elephants	trumpet	monkeys	chatter	swallows	twitter
frogs	croak	owls	hoot	turkeys	gobble

(A) What are the names of the noises made by these creatures?

(B) Write the missing words.

1 horses _____
2 oxen _____
3 bears _____
4 _____ gibber
5 _____ bellow
6 _____ chatter
7 _____ laugh
8 hounds _____
9 _____ chirp
10 _____ gobble

(C) Write the word needed to complete each sentence, adding **-ing** or **-ed** where required.

1 The pet lamb was _____ for more milk from the bottle.
2 The hounds were _____ with excitement.
3 When the bull _____ the children fled.
4 The continual _____ of the sparrows annoyed Elizabeth.
5 The parrot house at the zoo was filled with the _____ and _____ of these beautiful birds.
6 Judy, the elephant, _____ expectantly as her keeper approached with the food.
7 The old frog _____ contentedly as he hopped about on the edge of the pond.

JOHANN GUTENBERG

Imagine a world without books, newspapers, magazines and all the other printed material we take for granted today. People had none of these things before Johann Gutenberg invented the printing press in the fifteenth century. Although there were a few books available at that time, most people did not have access to them. Each book was handwritten by monks and it took months to produce a single copy. The books they produced were so rare and precious that they were locked away in monastery libraries.

Gutenberg was born in the German town of Mainz where his father was the Master of the Mint. The young boy was fascinated by the way the goldsmiths stamped letters and figures on to coins. Eventually, he became a skilled metalworker himself.

Gutenberg was also interested in the handwritten books in the monastery library. He would spend hours poring over them and watching the monks laboriously copying the scripts. As he watched, an idea came to him. Could a metalwork process be used to produce words on a page? Gutenberg's idea was to cut the letters of the alphabet on individual blocks of metal which could then be moved round to form words. He invented a printing press in which metal letters were fitted into a frame to make up the words on a page.

Gutenberg was a poor man and he needed money to develop his idea. Therefore, he agreed to a proposal put to him by a cunning lawyer named Johann Fust. Fust offered to pay for the printing press, inks and papers Gutenberg needed if he could become Gutenberg's partner.

In 1456, Gutenberg printed 300 copies of the famous *Gutenberg Bible*. This was the start of book publishing and should have made Gutenberg rich and famous. But Fust was greedy, and decided to get rid of his partner. He demanded his money back. Gutenberg could not pay, so Fust seized his equipment and took over the business. Gutenberg did not earn any money from his invention and died penniless twelve years later.

c. 1397	1428	1448	1450	1456	1468
born in Mainz, Germany	moves to Strasbourg and begins to experiment with printing apparatus	returns to Mainz and tries to borrow money for his work	forms partnership with Johann Fust and begins to set up printing press	prints 300 copies of the 1,282 page *Gutenberg Bible*	dies in Mainz

Twenty Inventors   Jacqueline Dineen

1 How were books produced before the printing press was invented?
2 Give two of the reasons why so few people had access to books before the printing press was invented.
3 Which two of Gutenberg's boyhood interests led to his invention?
4 What do you do if you **pore** over a book?
5 What does **laboriously** mean in paragraph three?
6 How was metal used in Gutenberg's printing press?
7 Fust and Gutenberg became partners in 1450. What did each contribute?
8 How many copies of the *Gutenberg Bible* were produced in 1456?
9 How many pages were there in the *Gutenberg Bible*?
10 In what way was Johann Fust greedy?
11 How much money did Gutenberg earn from his invention?
12 Suggest a heading for each paragraph that will accurately sum up what each is about.

SOUNDS

Object	Sound	Object	Sound
anvil	clang	engine	throb
bagpipes	skirl	explosion	blast
bell	peal; tinkle	hinges	creak
bow	twang	rifle	report
brakes	grinding	silk	rustle
bullet	ping	siren	wail
chains	jangle; rattle	skirts	swish
coins	chink; jingle	stream	babble; murmur
corks	pop	thunder	clap; peal
dishes	rattle; clatter	wings	whirr

(A) Write the missing words; some you learnt in Books 2 and 3.

1 the twang of a _____
2 the call of a _____
3 the tinkle of a _____
4 the jingle of _____
5 the shuffle of _____
6 the rustle of _____
7 the grinding of _____
8 the babble of a _____
9 the lash of a _____
10 the skirl of _____

11 the _____ of skirts
12 the _____ of dishes
13 the _____ of corks
14 the _____ of a bullet
15 the _____ of hoofs
16 the _____ of raindrops
17 the _____ of a rifle
18 the _____ of chains
19 the _____ of an anvil
20 a _____ of thunder

(B) Write in order the words necessary to complete these sentences.

1 With a noisy _____ of wings thousands of starlings descended on the town.
2 The bridal pair left the church to a merry _____ of bells.
3 The workmen were temporarily deafened by the _____ of the explosion.
4 The frequent _____ of the anvil showed how busy the blacksmith was.
5 When hinges _____ they require oiling.
6 The _____ of the siren announced that a fire had broken out.
7 The Highland regiment marched to the _____ of bagpipes.
8 Derek tossed restlessly in his bunk, disturbed by the _____ of the ship's engines.

DOERS OF ACTIONS

Memorize this list, then answer the questions.

Action	Doer	Action	Doer
apply	applicant	edit	editor
auction	auctioneer	guard	guardian
burgle	burglar	lie	liar
capture	captor	mutiny	mutineer
challenge	challenger	operate	operator
compete	competitor	oppose	opponent
contribute	contributor	preside	president
correspond	correspondent	represent	representative
criticize	critic	succeed	successor
dictate	dictator	survive	survivor

(A) What word is used for:

1 one who challenges?
2 one who contributes?
3 one who edits?
4 one who presides?
5 one who lies?

6 one who criticizes?
7 one who applies?
8 one who operates?
9 one who competes?
10 one who survives?

(B) Complete each sentence by inserting the word for the doer of the action.

1 A _____ broke into the bank last night. **burgle**
2 The young orphan was accompanied by his _____. **guard**
3 In two hours the _____ had sold all the paintings. **auction**
4 One _____ was shot in the chest. **mutiny**
5 The prisoner was treated well by his _____. **capture**
6 A _____ of the company demonstrated their computer software. **represent**
7 Some countries do not have a monarch or a president; they have a _____. **dictate**
8 in less than a minute the wrestler had thrown his _____. **oppose**
9 The retiring caretaker showed his _____ round the school. **succeed**
10 The film star ordered a photograph to be sent to every _____. **correspond**

THREE USES OF THE COMMA

Look at the examples below and see if you can work out **why** the commas have been used. Answers are on the right-hand side of the page.

Examples	*Reasons why commas are used*
1 *The last cottage we saw when we were house-hunting was a little one with thick walls and a squat chimney, and we both fell in love with it.*	**The comma provides a pause, a chance to get your breath back, in a long sentence.**
2 *Mrs Paul, our headmistress, is retiring this term.*	**The pair of commas encloses supplementary information about Mrs Paul. It could be omitted or put in brackets.**
3 a *The boys, who were wearing helmets, were not injured.*	**The pair of commas shows that all the boys are included** *No boy was injured.* *All the boys wore helmets.*
b *The boys who were wearing helmets were not injured.*	*Some boys were injured.* *Only those wearing helmets escaped.*

(A) Use one comma in each of these sentences to introduce a pause, (Look back later at the passage to see what the writers did.)

1 Modern agricultural methods include the use of pesticides which effectively control insects classified as pests but which also destroy many that are not. (Page 18)

2 Hounds swam beyond the line of waves while people stood at the sea-lap and watched the huntsman wading to his waist. (Page 66)

3 It swam slowly and with a great dark majesty out in the icy waters far away. (Page 60)

4 The church was very dark and quiet now but not empty because no place that has been used for so long by so many people can ever be empty. (Page 48)

5 Darzee and his wife only cowered down in the nest without answering for from the thick grass at the foot of the bush there came a low hiss – a horrid cold sound that made Rikki-tikki jump back two clear feet. (Page 24)

(B) Read this pair of sentences and answer the question that follows.

The girls who washed up were thanked by their teacher.
The girls, who washed up, were thanked by their teacher.

Which sentence means that *all* the girls were thanked because *all* the girls washed up?

(C) Copy these sentences, putting in the pair of commas needed in each to enclose supplementary information.

1 My dog a bulldog terrifies everyone.
2 The Prince the Queen's eldest son is heir to the throne.
3 The prize a trip to a theme park was won by the headmaster.
4 I had my favourite meal fish fingers and chips since it was my birthday.
5 Her best friend Zena Partridge is leaving.

A FIGHT IN A SIGNAL-TOWER

Up over the edge of the spur, three wild horsemen appeared heading for the gateway.

As they dropped from their ponies in the courtyard below, Marcus and Esca drew back from the parapet. "Only three, so far," Marcus whispered. "Don't use your knife unless you have to. They may be of more use to us living than dead."

Esca nodded, and returned his hunting-knife to his belt. Life and the urgency of doing had taken hold of them again. Flattened against the wall on either side of the stairhead they waited, listening to their pursuers questing through storehouse and guardroom. "Fools!" Marcus breathed, as a shout told them that the stairway had been spotted; and then came a rush of feet that checked at the floor below and then came on, storming upward.

Marcus was a good boxer, and much practice with the cestus last winter had made Esca something of a boxer also; together, weary though they were, they made a dangerous team. The first two tribesmen to come ducking out through the low doorway went down without a sound, like poled oxen; the third, not so completely caught unawares, put up more of a fight. Esca flung himself upon him, and they crashed down several steps together, in a flailing mass of arms and legs. There was a short, desperate struggle before Esca came uppermost, and staggering clear, heaved an unconscious man over the doorsill.

The Eagle of the Ninth   Rosemary Sutcliff

1 Where were Marcus and Esca when the horsemen appeared?
2 Where did the horsemen dismount?
3 Which words suggest there might have been more horsemen to come?
4 Why did Marcus advise Esca not to use his knife?
5 Where did Esca keep his knife?
6 Where were their pursuers searching for them?
7 Why did Marcus describe their pursuers as fools?
8 What kind of training had made Esca into a boxer?
9 Why did the third tribesman put up more of a fight than the other two?
10 In what state was the third tribesman after the fight?

DOUBLE NEGATIVES

Words containing **not** or **no** are called **negatives**.

no   not   nobody   nothing   nowhere   none   never (not ever)

Two negatives should never be used together in the same sentence.

Wrong

*He did **not** tell me **nothing** about it.* (two negatives)

Right

He did not tell me anything about it. (one negative)

*He told me **nothing** about it.* (one negative)

Choose the correct word from the pair above to complete each sentence.

1 nothing   anything
John did not tell his father _____ about the accident.
John told his father _____ about the accident.

2 nowhere   anywhere
We couldn't find the book _____.
The book was _____ to be found.

3 nothing   anything
The gardener didn't pay Tom _____ for his help.
The gardener paid Tom _____ for his help.

4 never   ever
Don't you _____ get tired of knitting?
Do you _____ get tired of knitting?

5 nothing   anything
We could not see _____ from where we stood.
We could see _____ from where we stood.

6 no   any
There isn't _____ cake left.
There is _____ cake left.

7 nobody   anybody
We didn't meet _____ on the way home.
We met _____ on the way home.

8 no   any
Haven't you _____ sympathy for him?
Have you _____ sympathy for him?

9 none   any
I asked Bill for a sweet but he didn't have _____.
I asked Bill for a sweet but he had _____.

10 no one   anyone
We can't find _____ to dig our garden.
We can find _____ to dig our garden.

11 nothing   anything
There isn't _____ wrong with this car.
There is _____ wrong with this car.

12 no   any
I looked everywhere but couldn't find _____ bluebells.
I looked everywhere but could find _____ bluebells.

MORE METAPHORS

Read this sentence and try to work out how the comparison between Miss James's voice and ice helps us to visualize the scene more clearly:

*Miss James spoke with an **icy** voice.*

The comparison makes the scene more vivid because we all know how cold ice makes us feel. We therefore know the effect of Miss James's voice on those listening.

Metaphors make descriptions more vivid because they compare something we know well with something we can then imagine and understand.

(A) All the examples of metaphors in the exercise below have been taken from passages in this book. You will have read most of them already. Now take the time to think carefully about how the metaphors help you to understand the descriptions better.

The metaphor in each sentence is in bold type. Explain how the metaphors help to make the descriptions more vivid.

1 The light **ebbed** from the church. (Page 48)
2 The fog came and went about it, momentarily **erasing** its shape. (Page 60)
3 "Thanks awfully, but I ought to **stick** by Toad till this trip is ended." (Page 12)
4 The strange fragrance was stronger now, coming over the top of the rise in a **wave** of scent that struck him powerfully. (Page 6)
5 The first two tribesmen to come **ducking** out through the low doorway went down without a sound. (Page 84)

(B) Look at each sentence below. From the three words in bold type above each sentence, choose the most appropriate metaphor. Then explain in your own words why the metaphor you have chosen is a good one.

1 flood   wavesurge
Tim felt a _____ of embarrassment when he saw all his friends were laughing at him.
2 enveloped   shrouded   parcelled
The graveyard was _____ in mist.
3 wolfed   pigged   gobbled
My dog Digger _____ all the sausages.
4 flew   sang   soared
As I got near home my heart _____ with excitement.

RHYMES

in	admire	thin	bigger	head	skin
kin	attire	pin	figure	red	chin

(A) Write the words, numbered from 1 to 12, which fill the spaces in this extract from a poem.

"Come in," the Mayor cried, looking _____: 1
And in did come the strangest _____! 2
His queer long coat from heel to _____, 3
Was half of yellow and half of _____, 4
And he himself was tall and _____, 5
With sharp blue eyes, each like a _____, 6
And light loose hair, yet swarthy _____, 7
No tuft on cheek, nor beard on _____, 8
But lips where smiles went out and _____; 9
There was no guessing his kith and _____ 10
And nobody could enough _____ 11
The tall man and his quaint _____. 12

(B) Each of these lines contains three rhyming words from which some of the letters are missing. Complete each word.

Example   **1** work
                      jerk
                      shirk

1 work   **4** home   **7** grows
   j _ _ _   f _ _ _   ch _ _ _
   sh _ _ _   c _ _ _   fr _ _ _
2 course   **5** become   **8** stole
   f _ _ _ _   cr _ _ _   sh _ _ _
   h _ _ _ _ _   gl _ _   scr _ _ _
3 nurse   **6** cheer   **9** bought
   v _ _ _ _   sm _ _ _   c _ _ _ _ _
   w _ _ _ _   sph _ _ _   t _ _ _

(C) Write as eight lines of poetry:
I have a garden of my own, shining with flowers of every hue; I loved it dearly while alone, but I shall love it more with you: and there the golden bees shall come in summer-time at break of morn, and wake us with their busy hum, around the Silea's fragrant thorn.

DIRECT SPEECH REVISION

Revise the punctuation of direct speech by looking at the examples below before you do the exercises.

Speech first

"I feel very tired," said Anne.

"Don't do that!" shouted Mark.

"Are you mad?" I asked.

Speech last

Anne said, "I feel very tired."

Mark shouted, "Don't do that!"

I asked, "Are you mad?"

An interrupted sentence of speech

"Nobody will ever know," he whispered, "what happened to the man."

A speech of more than one sentence

"I feel very tired. I am going to bed," said Anne.

Anne said, "I feel very tired. I am going to bed."

"I feel very tired," said Anne. "I am going to bed."

Dialogue

(Remember to start a new line for each new speaker.)

"Hi, Charles," said Stephen.

"Hi," said Charles.

"What are you doing?" asked Stephen.

"Nothing, really," replied Charles.

(A) Each sentence contains one punctuation error. Write the sentences correctly.

  1 "How are you?" Asked Anne.
  2 "I feel a bit sick" I said.
  3 "Would you like to lie down," she said kindly.
  4 The shopkeeper smiled and murmured "What can I do for you. madam?"
  5 "Just as we turned off the main road," said Elaine "a huge coach came roaring towards us!"

(B) Supply any missing punctuation marks and write out this conversation between Silver and Hazel, spacing it correctly. When you have finished, look at Page 6 to see how the author, Richard Adams, presented it.

Not asleep, Silver he said. It's too dangerous, Hazel replied Silver. I'd like to sleep as much as anyone but if we all sleep and something comes, who's going to spot it? I know. I've found a place where we can sleep safely for as long as we like. A burrow? No, not a burrow. A great field of scented plants that will cover us, sight and smell, until we're rested. Come out here and smell it, if you like.

IDIOMS

Learn this list of idioms and their meanings, then work the test which follows.

Idiom	Meaning
to send to Coventry	to ignore a person
to play second fiddle	to take a back place while someone else leads
to be at loggerheads	to be quarrelling
to make a mountain out of a molehill	to make trifling difficulties appear great ones
to feather one's nest	to increase one's possessions
to pay through the nose	to pay too high a price
to smell a rat	to be suspicious
to give a person the cold shoulder	to make him or her feel unwelcome
to blow one's own trumpet	to boast about oneself

Rewrite these sentences substituting for the words in bold type one of the **idioms** in the list.

1 Mr Robinson paid **far too high a price** for his car.
2 It is wrong to think only of **adding to one's possessions**.
3 Some people prefer **to take a back place and let someone else take the lead**.
4 Very soon the police began **to be suspicious**.
5 Alan is too fond of **boasting about himself**.
6 The two neighbours are forever **quarrelling**.
7 Faint-hearted people often like making **difficulties appear much greater than they really are**.
8 The bully's mates **ignored him and refused to talk to him**.
9 The old couple decided to give the tramp **the impression that he was most unwelcome**.

LONG JOHN SILVER

Long John Silver, our ship's cook - Barbecue, as the men called him – carried his crutch by a lanyard round his neck, to have both hands as free as possible. It was something to see him wedge the foot of his crutch against a bulkhead, and, propped against it, yielding to every movement of the ship, get on with his cooking like someone safe ashore. Still more strange was it to see him in the heaviest of weather cross the deck. He had a line or two rigged up to help him across the widest spaces, and he would hand himself from one place to another, as quickly as another man could walk.

"He's no common man, Barbecue," said the coxswain to me. "He had good schooling in his young days, and can speak like a book when so minded, and he's brave – a lion's nothing alongside of Long John! I've seen him grapple four men, and knock their heads together – and him unarmed."

All the crew respected and even obeyed him. He had a way of doing everybody some particular service. To me he was unweariedly kind; and always glad to see me in the galley.

"Hawkins," he would say, "come and have a yarn with John. Nobody more welcome than yourself, my son. Here's Cap'n Flint –I calls my parrot Cap'n Flint after the famous buccaneer – here's Cap'n Flint predicting success to our voyage. Wasn't you, cap'n?"

And the parrot would say, with great rapidity, "Pieces of eight! pieces of eight! pieces of eight!" till you wondered that it was not out of breath, or till John threw his handkerchief over the cage.

Treasure Island   Robert Louis Stevenson

1 What nickname did the crew give Long John Silver?
2 How did John carry his crutch?
3 Why did he carry it in this way?
4 How did he use his crutch when cooking?
5 What helped John to cross the widest spaces of the deck in the heaviest weather?
6 What example of John's bravery did the coxswain give?
7 Why did the crew respect John?
8 What was the name of John's parrot?
9 What is another word for "buccaneer"?
10 How did John stop the parrot talking?